Bodil Mortensen 9 or 10 year old Girl buried at Rock Creek Hollow
Funl work done by Pres. McKinnon who Pg 33/87

Pg 21 all to one Cart
Remember pg 75

THE SECOND RESCUE

THE SECOND RESCUE

The Story of the Spiritual Rescue of the Willie and Martin Handcart Pioneers

SUSAN ARRINGTON MADSEN

MILLENNIAL PRESS
OREM, UTAH

Library of Congress Cataloging-in-Publication Data
  Madsen, Susan Arrington.
    Second rescue / Susan Arrington Madsen.
      p.   cm.
    Includes bibliographical references and index.
    ISBN 1-932597-25-5
    1. Mormons—Wyoming—Biography.   2. Pioneers—Wyoming—Biography.
  3. Mormon Trail.   4. Temple work (Mormon Church)   5. Church of Jesus
Christ of Latter-day Saints.   Riverton Wyoming Stake—History.
  6. Mormon Church—Wyoming—Riverton Region—History.   7. Riverton
Region (Wyo.)—Church history.   8. Wyoming—Biography.   I. Title.
  BX8693.M327   1998
  289.3'092'2—dc21
  [B]
97-49662
                                        CIP

Printed in the United States of America

10 9 8 7 6 5 4 3 2 1   72082 - 6266

To the members of the Riverton Wyoming Stake,
The People of the Second Rescue

Blessed art thou, Nephi, for those things which thou hast done;
for I have beheld how thou hast with unwearyingness declared
the word, which I have given unto thee, unto this people. And
thou hast not feared them, and hast not sought thine own life, but
hast sought my will, and to keep my commandments.

And now, because thou hast done this with such unwearyingness,
behold, I will bless thee forever . . .

HELAMAN 10:4–5

CONTENTS

PREFACE

Occasionally an event or even a single moment comes along that significantly changes the way a person views the past. Such an event occurred for me on November 15, 1996. On that day, my husband, Dean, and I visited for the first time various sites in central Wyoming along the Mormon Trail. We were led by Robert Scott Lorimer, former president of the Riverton Wyoming Stake and guide extraordinaire for sites of particular significance to the James G. Willie and Edward Martin handcart companies of 1856.

After a chilly, breezy day of exploring Independence Rock, Devil's Gate, the Sun Ranch, and Martin's Cove, we headed for Rocky Ridge, some sixty-five miles to the west. It was there that my feelings, my empathy, for the weary and stranded pioneers sank especially deep.

Rocky Ridge is well named. Just as prophets, apostles, and other eager latter-day visitors have done, we drove up the steep, bumpy trail as far as we could go in President Lorimer's Suburban. With each jolt and swerve I asked myself, "How in the world did those exhausted, hungry, freezing souls get their carts and wagons up this rocky incline?"

On the day of our visit to Rocky Ridge, there were several inches of snow on the ground, making the trail even more forbidding. Twice the vehicle became stuck, and it was with some effort that we were able to push and shove the Suburban on its way again. The last time, about a half mile from the summit, President Lorimer suggested it would be best if the three of us walked the rest of the way. It was cold, it was still, and there was a beautiful moon in the sky as we walked and shared stories of the perilous situation that faced the Willie and Martin handcart pioneers in October of 1856. There was much talk of Captain Willie, Joseph Elder, and Ephraim Hanks. We also remembered Ann Rowley, Archibald McPhail, and little Mary Hurren.

Upon reaching the summit—at 7300 feet, one of the highest points along the entire Mormon Trail—we admired the monument built there by members of the Riverton Wyoming Stake. A few more stories, and it was time to return to the car. By then the scene had changed somewhat. The sky had clouded over, and the light of the moon was gone. Although we were dressed warmly, we had not remembered to bring a flashlight. It was very, very dark; no lights were to be seen in any direction.

For fifteen minutes, which somehow seemed much longer, we tried to find our way back to President Lorimer's Suburban. We missed one important turn and had to backtrack through the desolate, rocky terrain to find the right trail. We were alone in the blackness, in the middle of nowhere. The silence spoke volumes about our isolation, our exposure to the elements, our vulnerability. There was no help nearby and the wind was kicking up again.

Thanks to President Lorimer's intimate knowledge of the terrain, we soon found the car. It was a welcome sight. Within minutes we were driving back down the bumpy trail, munching on Dee Lorimer's famous chocolate-chip cookies, the warm heater humming. Safe again.

Our moment of uncertainty was ridiculously short compared to the weeks of terror and hardship experienced by hundreds of pioneer mothers and fathers. Mile after mile they comforted their little ones along the treacherous, snowy path. Death was constantly knocking at their door. As we drove through the darkness back to Riverton, President Lorimer apologized for the inconvenience on Rocky Ridge. I expressed to him, however, my deep gratitude for those few brief moments of isolation and fear. Because of those moments, I understand the strength and faith of the pioneers better now, and I love them even more.

That first trip to central Wyoming changed my life in other ways. I became acquainted, for example, with the people of the Riverton Wyoming Stake who participated in the project now known as the "Second Rescue." It has been a privilege to witness their humility, to feel their love for the handcart people, and to sense their gratitude for being involved in this sacred, Spirit-led project. It has been an honor to compile a book on their experiences. Many sacred and memorable stories were given to me that could not be included in the final book. Those stories are forever recorded in the hearts and souls of those who participated.

Several excellent books and hundreds of fine articles have been published on the Mormon handcart experience. This book does not attempt to duplicate their contributions. Instead, *The Second Rescue* tells how the Lord led the present-day Saints of the Riverton Wyoming Stake to discover that more than half of the temple ordinances for those heroic 1856 pioneers and their families were not yet done. It also describes their discovery of what the Lord wanted the Wyoming Saints to do about it, and what the remarkable fruits of their obedience to the Spirit were.

In this book, representative stories of the Willie, Martin, Hunt, and Hodgett companies of 1856 appear as sidebars alongside the main text. Stories of the faith and sacrifice of these early pioneers are included because they are important to our understanding of the spiritual significance of the Second Rescue. These accounts will also help those who read the book understand the deep love and attachment the people who participated in the Second Rescue feel for these remarkable pioneers.

My role has been that of compiler, abridger, and storyteller. President R. Scott Lorimer, untiring in his efforts, has provided me with the equivalent of a small truckload of materials from which to tell this remarkable story. He has promptly answered my many letters, phone calls, and questions, enabling me to clarify the text and forge ahead with the writing of the manuscript. He has served as advisor, editor, and cheerleader for this project. He loves the people of the Riverton Wyoming Stake, and has a deep and very personal love for the pioneers.

Others who have provided valuable insights and materials for this book have been President Lorimer's counselors, President John L. Kitchen, Jr., and President Kim W. McKinnon. Diane McKinnon worked many hours gathering and organizing photographs. Donna Olsen, secretary to the Riverton Wyoming Stake presidency, generously provided the rosters of the Willie and Martin handcart companies and the Hunt and Hodgett wagon companies that appear in the appendix. She also provided pioneer stories, allowed me the use of her personal journal, and answered many questions concerning the 1856 pioneers. Material describing the involvement of the Ogden Utah Temple Presidency, staff, and volunteer temple workers was read and approved by Dorman Baird, who was serving as Ogden Temple president at the time of the Second Rescue, and Robert Memmott, Ogden Temple recorder.

Unless otherwise indicated, photographs were provided by members of the Riverton Wyoming Stake. Source citations refer mostly to materials collected in the Riverton Wyoming Stake Handcart Library. Some journals and transcripts of oral interviews are in private possession.

The story of the Second Rescue will touch the hearts of all who seek to live by the Spirit. In a powerful way, it teaches the importance of families, the significance of temple work, and the workings of the Lord in our daily lives. It is a story that will be especially dear to those who make the journey to Wyoming and sense a feeling of love and triumph at the rescue sites in that rugged land. My greatest desire is to help impart to the reader the powerful spirit of this unique and moving chapter in American history.

People are often surprised when they learn that I have no Mormon pioneer ancestry. My paternal grandparents, Noah and Edna Corn Arrington, came west on a train in 1913, eventually settling near Twin Falls, Idaho. My mother, Grace, a North Carolina convert to The Church of Jesus Christ of Latter-day Saints, "crossed the plains" in 1946 in an automobile named "Mr. Bill." She and my father drove from Raleigh to Logan, Utah, where my father had accepted a position in economics at Utah State Agricultural College, later known as Utah State University.

So, on that day in November 1996 when Dean and I visited the Mormon Trail sites in central Wyoming, I was not retracing the steps of my own ancestors. I was making a pilgrimage, building bridges to the souls of many pioneers, living and dead, whom I have come to consider my dear friends. It would be impossible for me to measure the ways their physical and spiritual sacrifices have blessed my life. Suffice it to say that I will be eternally grateful for what I have felt and learned at their feet.

Susan Arrington Madsen
Hyde Park, Utah

CHAPTER 1

AN EARLY OCTOBER SNOWSTORM

"A condition of distress here met my eyes that I never saw before or since."
DANIEL W. JONES, 1856 RESCUER

A HOWLING OCTOBER SNOWSTORM BLINDED ten-year-old Bodil Mortensen as she climbed with several other younger children, shivering and hungry, up the snow-covered slope of Rocky Ridge. The high plains of Wyoming had not been kind to Mormon handcart pioneers in the late fall of 1856. For some, the ascent westward over South Pass was this life's final test.

Bodil's older sister, Margaret, had crossed the plains and mountains to Utah the previous year. The girls' parents, Niels and Maren Hansen Mortensen, and other siblings were still in Denmark, planning to make the journey as soon as funds were available. The family was too poor to send everyone at once.

Bodil was traveling in the care of her parents' friends Jens and Else Nielsen and their son, Niels. In April they had said good-bye to Bodil's family in Denmark, traveled by ship to England, and taken a train to the great port city of Liverpool.

In Liverpool they boarded a three-masted sailing vessel, the *Thornton*, along with 761 others who had joined The Church of Jesus Christ of Latter-day Saints. The *Thornton* sailed on May 4, 1856, under the leadership of Elder James G. Willie, a missionary returning from England. Six weeks at sea brought the converts to New York City. Traveling by steamboat and in railway boxcars outfitted with benches, they journeyed inland to Iowa City. There they prepared for their handcart trek west and were assigned to the fourth handcart company of the season, led by Captain Willie.

PATIENCE LOADER ROZSA ARCHER

The James and Amy Loader family worked in New York for several months before making their way to Iowa. When asked to joined the Edward Martin handcart company, Patience expressed some concern:

"This was a terrible great surprise to us all. At first we felt we never could undertake to pull a handcart from Iowa to Salt Lake City and my poor mother in delicate health. She had not walked a mile for years and we girls had never been used to outdoor work. I think I felt the worst out of all the family. I could not see it right at all to want us to do such a humiliating thing. To be . . . harnessed up like cattle and pull a handcart loaded up with our bedding, cooking utensils, and our food and clothing, and have to go through different towns to be looked at and made fun of as I knew we would be. It was very hurtful to my feelings; yes, I will say to my pride."

But like so many others, they went anyway, leaving Iowa on July 28, 1856, and then Florence, Nebraska, on August 27th.

"Diary of Patience Loader Rosa [Rozsa] Archer." Typescript, Harold B. Lee Library, Brigham Young University, Provo, Utah.

Captain James G. Willie.
Photograph courtesy
Paul Willie.

It was late in the season. Not until July 15 were they able to leave Iowa City, and by August 11 they had made it only as far as Florence, Nebraska, near present-day Omaha. Delays in travel and in the construction of handcarts put them far behind their intended schedule. On August 13, a council was held in which the views of those who favored continuing to Zion that year were expressed. However, Levi Savage, an experienced frontiersman, warned of the potential dangers of such a course. He felt sure that it would be impossible to cross the mountains so late in the season without a great deal of suffering, sickness, and death. After the discussion, a vote was taken, and the fateful decision was made to press on immediately to the Salt Lake Valley. To his credit, Savage then offered everything he had to help the group:

"Brethren and sisters, what I have said I know to be true; but, seeing you are to go forward, I will go with you, will help you all I can, will work with you, will rest with you, will suffer with you, and, if necessary, I will die with you. May God in his mercy bless and preserve us." (John Chislett narrative published in T. B. H. Stenhouse, *The Rocky Mountain Saints* [New York: D. Appleton, 1873].)

On August 16, 1856, Bodil and about 500 others in the Willie company continued their journey westward. Nearly 600 souls in the Edward Martin handcart company, as well as a total of approximately 450 in the John A. Hunt and William B. Hodgett wagon trains, followed within two weeks. (See LeRoy R. Hafen and Ann W. Hafen, *Handcarts to Zion, 1856–1860* [Glendale, Calif.: The Arthur H. Clark Company, 1960], p. 93.)

The trek proceeded across present-day Nebraska. It was not until the company was in Wyoming that the first signs of impending disaster appeared. Temperatures plummeted and the pioneers' clothing and tents proved inadequate for the freezing weather. Provisions ran short and there was no way to replenish them.

On October 5, 1856, messengers informed Brigham Young in Salt Lake City that there were nearly 1,600 souls still out on the high plains of Wyoming and their circumstances were desperate. Within two days, at Brigham Young's urging, the first of many rescue parties left Salt Lake City in a courageous effort that would span more than two months.

And then came the snow. Heavy winter storms began a month earlier than usual. The snowfall slowed the travel of little Bodil Mortensen and the Willie handcart company, then delayed it, and finally brought it to a terrifying halt.

By October 20, 1856, the members of the Willie handcart company, Bodil among them, were camped by the Sweetwater River, not far from the base of Rocky Ridge. The cold was intense. A week earlier flour rations had been reduced to ten and a half ounces per day for men, nine ounces for women, six ounces for children, and three ounces for infants. Supplies were dwindling fast.

In the midst of the storm, Captain Willie and Joseph B. Elder, riding a pony and a mule, crossed Rocky Ridge looking for the rescue party they knew to be on the way. Riding in what was often a complete whiteout, they prayed they would not lose the road. They found the rescuers ten miles past the summit, waiting out the storm at Rock Creek Hollow. The rescuers were unsure where the Willie company was, or indeed whether anyone could survive the weather. Notwithstanding the storm, fourteen rescue wagons were quickly hitched up and driven through the blowing snow toward the Willie company, who were camped near the Sweetwater River, shivering and out of food. The rescuers arrived two days later, on October

GEORGE CUNNINGHAM

George describes his experiences with the Willie handcart company:

"The nights now began to get very cold and feed was poor, also our provisions were running out fast. Starvation looked us in the face. We were put on rations of six ounces of flour each per day and nothing else. The old and the weak began to die for want of proper food, and a great many of the young and strong ones soon followed suit. I, myself, have helped to bury ten to fifteen in a single day. We who could stand it were barely kept alive and after several weeks of this ration [of flour] it was reduced to half this amount. I, however, stirred my three ounces with some water and gulped it down.

" . . . We used to boil the bones and drink the soup. Every particle that could be used was taken, even the hide was rationed and after scorching the hair off, we would roast it a little over the coals and cut it in small pieces and it made what we considered a delicious supper.

" . . . We built large fires with willows which were abundant at this place. Everybody stood around the fire with gloomy faces, as if in a death trap."

George Cunningham, in "The Handcart Pioneers," in Kate B. Carter, comp., *Treasures of Pioneer History*, 6 vols. Salt Lake City: Daughters of Utah Pioneers, 1956, 5:252–56.

JOHN CHISLETT

"The storm which we encountered, our [rescuers] from the [Salt Lake] Valley also met, and, not knowing that we were so utterly destitute, they encamped to await fine weather. But when Captain Willie found them and explained our real condition, they at once hitched up their teams and made all speed to come to our rescue.

"On the evening of the third day after Captain Willie's departure, just as the sun was sinking beautifully behind the distant hills, on an eminence immediately west of our camp, several covered wagons, each drawn by four horses, were seen coming towards us. The news ran through the camp like wildfire, and all who were able to leave their beds turned out en masse to see them. A few minutes brought them sufficiently near to reveal our faithful Captain slightly in advance of the train. Shouts of joy rent the air; strong men wept till tears ran freely down their furrowed and sun-burnt cheeks, and little children partook of the joy which some of them hardly understood, and fairly danced around with gladness."

John Chislett narrative published in T.B.H. Stenhouse, *The Rocky Mountain Saints*. New York: D. Appleton, 1873.

22. The Willie company kept six of the wagons to supply their 500 people and sent the remaining eight wagons to the aid of the Saints in the Martin handcart company and the Hunt and Hodgett wagon trains, more than eighty miles farther east, near Horse Creek.

The handcart pioneers were in a very weakened condition. What lay immediately ahead for the Willie Saints was the treacherous ascent of Rocky Ridge to the summit, and then the trek on to the camp at Rock Creek Hollow. The distance was about twelve miles, including a two-mile stretch in which the trail rose more than 700 feet in elevation. The snow was already more than a foot deep, a blizzard was raging, and temperatures were far below freezing.

Ten-year-old Bodil Mortensen made that twelve-mile journey with the rest of the Willie company on October 23, 1856. The forced march took some of the pioneers twenty-seven hours, slogging through the snow, making an average of less than one-half mile per hour. While adults wrestled handcarts up the steep trail, Bodil and the younger children fought their way through the snow, wind, and freezing temperatures to get to Rock Creek.

Exhausted and weak, the intrepid young Danish girl closed her eyes for the last time that day. Her frozen little body was later found by company members; her spirit was now in a safe, warm place.

Bodil was buried in a common grave with twelve others who also died that night. Before the thirteen bodies were covered, James Hurren held up his eight-year-old daughter, Mary, to let her see one of her playmates lying among the dead. Two men who helped dig the grave died a few hours later and were buried nearby. Their sacrifice has forever made Rock Creek Hollow, in central Wyoming, a sacred place.

The Willie handcart company journeyed on and, with the help of the tireless rescuers, arrived in the Salt Lake Valley on November 9, 1856. The

Martin handcart company arrived on November 30, and the last of the Hunt and Hodgett wagons rolled into Salt Lake City on December 15.

Among these four companies, more than 220 Saints died. The rescue initiated by Brigham Young mobilized the meager resources of the Utah Saints and in heroic fashion ultimately saved the lives of more than 1,300 men, women, and children, most of whom would otherwise surely have perished.

Time passed—135 years, to be exact. Generation succeeded generation. Led by prophets, the church and kingdom of God continued to grow. Stakes, wards, and branches took root throughout the world, and temples dotted the earth.

On August 14, 1991, in one of those sacred houses of the Lord, the name of the little Danish girl, Bodil Mortensen, was spoken again, reverently and authoritatively. On that day, Sarah Lorimer, age fifteen, entered the Ogden Temple in Utah and was baptized for and in behalf of Bodil. Another Riverton Wyoming Stake member, Diane Isom McKinnon, served there as proxy to receive instruction and make covenants that would reach out over time and generations to bless Bodil's eternal life.

And finally, culminating that sacred day in the Ogden Temple, Scott Lorimer and his wife, Dee, knelt across an altar alongside Ruth Mortensen Hauck, the three acting as proxies for Bodil and her father and mother. They reverently participated in a sacred sealing ordinance that would unite Bodil with her parents for eternity.

Scott Lorimer later wrote of that day in the temple: "There were times when I knew if I would just look up I would be able to see the pioneers. They have a tremendous spirit. President Dorman Baird, president of the Ogden Temple, had trouble throughout the sealing ceremony. He became overcome with emotion and had to stop for a long time. . . . He concluded the sealing ceremony and said, 'These people are certainly accepting what

JOHN JAQUES

"The meeting of the emigrants with relatives, acquaintances, and friends . . . was very solemnly impressive. Some were so affected that they could scarcely speak, but would look at each other until the sympathetic tears would force their unforbidden way. In a short time, however, the emigrants were taken into the homes of their friends and made as comfortable as circumstances would permit them to be while they thawed the frost out of their limbs and recruited their health and strength. The new comers would eat and eat and eat until they were literally and perfectly ashamed of themselves, and then retire from the table hungry. It took a long time for an emigrant to fill up and reduce his appetite to its normal condition. It was a serious affliction upon those who had it, as well as upon their hospitable friends."

Stella Jaques Bell, ed., *Life History and Writings of John Jaques, including a Diary of the Martin Handcart Company.* Rexburg, Idaho: Ricks College Press, 1978, p. 172. This volume consists largely of Jaques's "Reminiscences," serialized in the *Salt Lake Daily Herald,* 1878–79.

we are doing here today.' Later, he thanked us for allowing him and the Ogden Temple to do these 'precious names.'" (Lorimer Journal.)

How and why Scott Lorimer, his family, and others from the Riverton Wyoming Stake came to be at the temple that day in behalf of Bodil Mortensen and others is the substance of this book. The story that follows is one of courage, personal revelation, and divine providence. It is the story of how the hearts of living Saints were turned by the spirit of the prophet Elijah to those who had gone before, bringing blessings to both the living and the dead.

CHAPTER 2

THE DOCTRINE

"A voice of gladness for the living and the dead . . . "
DOCTRINE AND COVENANTS 128:19

To FULLY APPRECIATE THE SPIRIT OF ELIJAH and the meaning of the project that would soon face members of the Riverton Wyoming Stake, one must first understand the basic doctrines that draw Latter-day Saints to the temples of the Lord. The passion and sacrifice that those Saints invested in their task can be understood only in the context of the urgency of performing temple ordinances.

The words *genealogy* and *family history* refer to the study of family and the identification of lines of descent. As members of The Church of Jesus Christ of Latter-day Saints, the people of the Riverton Wyoming Stake had long been taught a commitment to principles of family history and genealogy rooted in the Bible and modern-day revelation.

The last two verses of the Old Testament, in the book of Malachi, proclaim: "Behold, I will send you Elijah the prophet before the coming of the great and dreadful day of the Lord: And he shall turn the heart of the fathers to the children, and the heart of the children to their fathers, lest I come and smite the earth with a curse." (Malachi 4:5–6.)

Although the Bible does not contain an explanation of the exact nature of the mission of Elijah, Latter-day Saints received that understanding line upon line, precept upon precept, in the nineteenth century. Those same verses from the book of Malachi, with slight variation, were quoted to Joseph Smith by Moroni during that heavenly messenger's first visit to the boy prophet.

Joseph Smith received visions and many revelations that eventually led to the organization of the

ANN JEWELL ROWLEY

Ann Jewell Rowley was a widow when she crossed the plains with the Willie handcart company. Her husband, William, had died in 1848. Ann relates her story:

"I was left a widow with 7 children under 12 years of age and the step children of William's first marriage. I was very grateful for the gospel of Jesus Christ and the comfort it gave me. I knew that our parting was only temporary and that viewed from the eternities, this was but a fleeting moment. I also knew that no matter how fleeting a moment it was, I had to make the best of it. I had a very real job to do. The children had to be fed and clothed, but the big task and the one I must accomplish, is to get us all to Zion. I must be among the people of my faith and I must get the Temple work done for us. Each person that could earn money at all, was required to work."

Autobiography of Ann Jewell Rowley, in James Albert Jones, *Some Early Pioneers of Huntington, Utah and Surrounding Area,* 1980, 241–47.

Church. Among those visions were visits from heavenly beings who restored the priesthood. In 1829, John the Baptist appeared to Joseph Smith and Oliver Cowdery and restored the Priesthood of Aaron, which included the authority to baptize. Later, the Apostles Peter, James, and John restored the Melchizedek, or higher, Priesthood.

Included in this restoration of all things was the merciful and glorious doctrine of salvation for the dead. Joseph Smith explained that when Malachi foretold the return of Elijah, he "had his eye fixed on the restoration of the priesthood, the glories to be revealed in the last days, and in an especial manner this *most glorious of all subjects* belonging to the everlasting gospel, namely, the baptism [salvation] for the dead." (Doctrine and Covenants 128:17; emphasis added.)

This same revelation proclaims that the restoration of the gospel is therefore to be seen as "glad tidings for the dead; a voice of gladness for the living and the dead; glad tidings of great joy." (Verse 19.)

Latter-day Saints believe that baptism, together with the laying on of hands for the gift of the Holy Ghost, is essential to salvation. Many early Saints, therefore, worried about the salvation of family members and dear friends who had died with no chance to accept the restored gospel or to be baptized by someone holding the priesthood. This concern was joyfully resolved in subsequent years in connection with the building of the first latter-day temples.

In 1832, Joseph Smith received a revelation in which the Lord commanded the Saints to build a temple that would become "a house of prayer, a house of fasting, a house of faith, a house of learning, a house of glory, a house of order, a house of God." (Doctrine and Covenants 88:119.) This temple was built in Kirtland, Ohio, and its dedication in 1836 was accompanied by numerous visions and spiritual outpourings.

Of particular importance was a manifestation on April 3, 1836. Joseph Smith and Oliver Cowdery retired to the pulpit at the west end of the second floor of the Kirtland Temple. Drawing a curtain for privacy, they knelt in humble prayer. "The veil was taken from our minds," they later wrote, "and the eyes of our understanding were opened. We saw the Lord standing upon the breastwork of the pulpit, before us." (Doctrine and Covenants 110:1–2.) In speaking to Joseph and Oliver, the Lord accepted the temple and foretold its influence among generations of people throughout the world. Other visions opened, and then, at long last, the following:

" . . . Another great and glorious vision burst upon us; for Elijah the prophet, who was taken to heaven without tasting death, stood before us, and said:

"Behold, the time has fully come, which was spoken of by the mouth of Malachi—testifying that he [Elijah] should be sent, before the great and dreadful day of the Lord come—

"To turn the hearts of the fathers to the children, and the children to the fathers, lest the whole earth be smitten with a curse—

"Therefore, the keys of this dispensation are committed into your hands; and by this ye may know that the great and dreadful day of the Lord is near, even at the doors." (Doctrine and Covenants 110:13–16.)

Elijah appears to Joseph Smith and Oliver Cowdery in the Kirtland Temple. Painting by Robert T. Barrett. Used by permission.

Elijah had come, fulfilling the prophecy of Malachi. With the restoration of the necessary keys, Latter-day Saints began to perform proxy baptisms for their deceased family members in 1840. The first such baptisms were performed in the Mississippi River, near Nauvoo, Illinois, where the Saints had relocated following persecutions in Ohio and Missouri. Soon thereafter, Joseph Smith received revelation that the Saints should again build a temple, this time in Nauvoo. Furthermore, the revelation declared, a temple dedicated as a House of the

Lord would be hereafter the proper place to perform vicarious baptisms.

The Kirtland Temple.
© 1997 David and LaRene Gaunt.

Baptism was not the only temple ordinance to be performed for the deceased. Worthy Latter-day Saints were also to receive the "endowment," special instruction and the making of sacred covenants to help prepare the individual for exaltation in the Lord's eternal kingdom. The Prophet Joseph Smith also taught that marriage bonds should last forever. A marriage performed by priesthood authority recognized by God would last through eternity, and the children from such a marriage would be part of an eternal family union. Temple ordinances creating such eternal family bonds became known as "sealings."

Church members have been taught since the time of Joseph Smith that these ordinances can and should be performed for both the living and the dead, and that such ordinances are necessary to form connecting links within families, ultimately uniting families with their earthly progenitors all the way back to our first parents, Adam and Eve.

Joseph Smith felt great urgency concerning the salvation of the dead. Less than three months before his death in 1844, he warned, "The greatest responsibility in this world that God has laid upon us is to seek after our dead." (*History of the Church*, 6:313.)

Of course, interest among Church members in performing sacred ordinances for their kindred dead did not stop with the death of the Prophet Joseph Smith. Under the guidance of a divinely inspired succession of modern-day prophets, Latter-day Saints have continued to build temples throughout the world and to seek out the names, birthdates, and other information needed to bring the full blessings of the gospel to deceased family members and friends.

The Church has invested enormous amounts of faith, time, talent, money, and facilities in this sacred work. Under Church sponsorship, the Genealogical Society of Utah was formed in 1894. Its charter members contributed eleven volumes of records. From that small beginning has grown a world-renowned family history library in Salt Lake City, Utah, housing hundreds of thousands of volumes and millions of reels of micro-filmed records from all over the world. Row upon row of computers now use the latest technology to help patrons with their research. A large staff of professional family history researchers as well as specially trained mis-sionaries help people of all faiths search out their roots.

In addition to the main library in Salt Lake City, the Church has estab-lished more than 3,000 small family history centers throughout the world. Each center is open to the public and has its own collection of research materials as well as the capacity to order films and other records from the main library in Salt Lake City.

In 1990, two such branch libraries lay within the boundaries of the Riverton Wyoming Stake of The Church of Jesus Christ of Latter-day Saints. The work that would be accomplished at those two stake family history libraries would soon change the lives of hundreds of Saints on both sides of the veil.

CHAPTER 3

THE WILLIE PROJECT BEGINS

*"I did not receive an answer, but rather an understanding that I was
on the right track and that I was to continue."*
PRESIDENT R. SCOTT LORIMER

ROBERT SCOTT LORIMER GREW UP IN CASPER, Wyoming. As a boy, he had heard his mother talk about her grandfather Niels Peter Ipson, who made the long trek from Iowa City, Iowa, to the Salt Lake Valley with the Daniel D. McArthur handcart company in 1856.

While attending Junior Sunday School in the 1950s, "Scotty" was captivated by the pioneer stories his teacher, Rhea White, told her class of young Latter-day Saints. One Sunday, Sister White showed the children a picture of the handcart pioneers camped in Martin's Cove. The painting depicted a young boy looking at a man lying on the ground, with his family huddled in sorrow around him. Sister White explained that the man had worked very hard and died. She turned to Scotty and asked what he thought the boy in the painting was looking at. He replied, "His boots." She asked him if he would have taken the boots off the feet of the deceased man if he had been there. It was a difficult question for a young man to answer. After a long pause, Scotty responded, "I guess he doesn't need them anymore." Sister White had the children look more closely at the boots and said that there was a lot of wear left in them. She agreed that the man didn't need them anymore and that he would surely want someone else to use them. This was Scott Lorimer's introduction to the Willie and Martin handcart pioneers. Something inside his soul had been stirred, and he would never be the same.

Years later, while working on a graduate degree at the University of Nebraska, Scott learned from an acquaintance of the existence of a Willie handcart company burial site in an area called Rock Creek Hollow near Atlantic City, Wyoming. He was more than just casually interested in locating the spot; something seemed to nag at him to find the secluded pioneer graves.

In 1976, Scott accepted a job opportunity and moved with his family to Riverton, Wyoming. On July 4, 1977, after inquiring among local Riverton stake members as to the location of the burial site, he visited Rock Creek Hollow with his family, fellow Church member Donna Gard, and others. Donna was one of the few people in the Riverton area who knew the location of the isolated trail site and something of its significance. She had visited there as a child.

"The Hand-cart Emigrants in a Storm," in T. B. H. Stenhouse, The Rocky Mountain Saints *(New York: D. Appleton, 1873), p. 310.*

While at Rock Creek, Scott imagined the cold, hunger, and desperation experienced by members of the Willie handcart company who camped there after the most harrowing and dangerous one-day trek of the entire journey. The twelve-mile march up Rocky Ridge and down to Rock Creek Hollow in snow, wind, and freezing temperatures proved to be too great a challenge for some. John Chislett, a member of the company, helped care for the dead. He wrote in his journal the day after the march:

"In the forenoon I was appointed to go round the camp and collect the dead. I took with me two young men to assist me in the sad task, and we collected together, of all ages and both sexes, thirteen corpses, all stiffly frozen. We had a large square hole dug in which we buried these thirteen people, 3 or 4 abreast and 3 deep. When they did not fit in, we put one or two crosswise at the head or feet of the others. We covered them with willows and then with the earth. . . . Two others died during the day, and we buried them in one grave, making fifteen in all buried on that camp ground." (John Chislett narrative, in Stenhouse, *Rocky Mountain Saints.*)

Scott sensed the sacredness of Rock Creek Hollow and had a great desire to share that sacred feeling with others. "Immediately when I went on the property I felt a very strong spirit there," he said. "As a newly called counselor in the stake presidency, I asked the stake president at the time, DeMar Taylor, if we could begin holding Pioneer Day celebrations at Rock Creek Hollow. The Riverton stake didn't hold Pioneer Day celebrations back then. Of course, we don't get July 24th off as a holiday in Wyoming. But I asked, nonetheless, if we could do that. He was a bit hesitant, but then agreed. His only hesitation was that it was a bit out of the way. He was concerned that not many people would come. But he did agree." (Lorimer Oral History, p. 2.)

Youth pull handcarts over Rocky Ridge during a 1980 handcart trek.

The first pioneer celebration at Rock Creek Hollow, held in 1979, was a great success for the most part. President Wendell Bunnell, a past member of the Riverton stake presidency, served as chairman. The "authentic pioneer dinner" of homemade whole-wheat bread, milk, and raw onions didn't sit well with some, but, in spite of the evening meal, everyone agreed it was a fitting and memorable activity in honor of the pioneers.

Another tradition that served to connect members of the stake with their pioneer heritage came as a result of obedience to Church leaders. Following the counsel of their Area President, Elder Loren C. Dunn, Riverton Wyoming Stake President DeMar Taylor instructed his counselors and the stake Young Men and Young Women presidencies to look for a place within their stake boundaries to hold youth conferences to avoid excessive travel and expense. Their obedience resulted in plans to organize a handcart trek for the youth at Oregon Buttes, finding treasures "in their own backyard."

While preparing for the trek, the young people quickly empathized with the original handcart pioneers as they attempted to build suitable handcarts. They constructed several carts using donated boards from an old granary that had been torn down. The handcarts did not travel far before they completely disintegrated, the sturdiest among them lasting only two miles. But the teenagers still had a great time singing, bearing testimony, and square dancing out on the windy plains of Wyoming.

Handcart treks for the Riverton stake youth continued to be held every four years. With each trek, the participants showed more enthusiasm and more humility as their knowledge of the suffering of the handcart pioneers increased. The teenagers anxiously awaited their turn to pull carts up over Rocky Ridge and on to Rock Creek Hollow.

The lives of the youth who participated in these treks were influenced in significant ways. For example, Brian Parry, age fourteen, wrote: "My feelings started when I was five miles into the handcart trek. My friend and I were beginning to feel a bit tired. We started talking about how much harder the pioneers had it having to walk on the same terrain but with two feet of snow and freezing temperatures to go with it. My heart went out to those courageous and brave people."

Aaron J. Moulton, age fourteen, who had ancestors in the Willie handcart company, wrote: "On the trek the desert was very hot during the day. The night was very cold and I liked my sleeping bag. I wondered how my great-great-grandparents survived the trek. I have grown to know and appreciate them. I have become familiar with the sacrifices they made in coming across the plains. I know that my ancestors sacrificed a lot to live in the promised land. There is a neat spirit walking on the trails that the pioneers took across the plains. I hope that I can remember this experience and share it with my family often."

Matthew Bills, who was too young to go on a trek, dreamed of his own chance to participate: "I like the handcarts that my brother and sister were pushing. When I get big I want to push a handcart."

Parents of those who participated saw a change in their teenagers who

JOHN JAQUES

"One man's hand-cart broke down one afternoon in the hills, and by some mischance the company all went on, leaving him behind, alone with his broken cart and his and his family's little stock of worldly goods thereon. He was drawing his little child in his cart, as he had drawn her most of the journey, and as he subsequently drew her to the last crossing of the Platte, but when his cart broke down he had to transfer her to somebody else's cart and send her on with the company. So he remained behind with his cart, anxiously expecting somebody to turn back and help him, but no one came. Night drew on apace, and still he was all alone, save and excepting the presence of a prowling wolf, which could be seen in the streak of light on the western horizon, a little outside of ordinary rifle range. Happily, just as darkness was settling down, Captain Hodgett's wagon company was observed coming down the opposite hill, from the east, at the base of which it encamped, a quarter or half a mile distant from the benighted and lonely hand-cart; he eagerly went and told his tale of misfortune to the wagon people, and they took him in for the night."

Stella Jaques Bell, ed., *Life History and Writings of John Jaques, including a Diary of the Martin Handcart Company*. Rexburg, Idaho: Ricks College Press, 1978.

LEVI SAVAGE

"Ascended Rocky Ridge. It was a severe day. The wind blew awful hard and cold. The ascent was some five miles long in places, steep, and covered with deep snow. We became weary and sat down to rest, and some became chilled and commenced to freeze. I returned to camp and found men, women and children, sitting and shivering with cold, around their small fires. Two teams started to bring up the rear, just before daylight, with dying and some dead. It was certainly heartrending to hear children crying for their mothers, and mothers crying for their children."

Levi Savage, Journal. Typescript, Utah State University, Logan, Utah.

experienced the ordeal. Ilene Olsen wrote: "When my son left on the trek, he was unsure of many things, especially of himself and of his testimony of the truthfulness of the gospel. When he and I met along with the rest of the family the next day on South Pass, he was a different person. He had a light in his soul which I had not seen for a long time, and a burning testimony to go with it. He has made such progress since then, as has the rest of our family."

Adults experiencing the treks were moved with compassion for the pioneers who endured the long ordeal of walking toward Zion more than a century and a half earlier. Teri Toland was deeply affected while visiting Rocky Ridge, the most difficult part of the trek for the Willie handcart pioneers: "I could imagine how the company slowly wound their way up the hill. There must have been so many words of encouragement, so many pains to bear from the body and soul. At what point would my faith have faltered? What thoughts must have gone through their minds? It is hard to imagine being so close to death with only one's faith to rely on. There was absolutely nothing but more mountains, more snow, more wind and cold. There was no relief in sight. I truly found a special place in my heart for those valiant souls."

Clearly, when the Riverton Wyoming Stake presidency was reorganized in September of 1987, the hearts of many stake members had already been turned toward the handcart pioneers.

Thirty-six-year-old Scott Lorimer was called as the new stake president that fall. He had already served for nine years as a counselor in the stake presidency. John L. Kitchen, Jr., and Kim W. McKinnon were called to serve as his counselors. President Lorimer continued to have a gnawing feeling that the "Willie people," as he affectionately called the 1856 handcart pioneers, had a project in mind for the members of his stake.

"I felt a very strong urging to ask the people of the stake to pray about the 'Willie Project.' That's what I asked them to do, to pray about the Willie

Project. And I had no idea what I was even asking them to do. In retrospect I sometimes thought, 'My word, what have I done?' I would hear little children who couldn't even say *Willie* praying about the Willie Project, and old people, too. They were just obedient to their stake president. (Lorimer Oral History, p. 3.)

What was the Willie Project? The spirit nearly everyone felt at Rock Creek Hollow and the importance of the historical events that had taken place there suggested that the Church ought to make efforts to acquire the land. Inquiries were made, but the owner was asking a very high price. Plans to purchase the land were temporarily set aside.

The stake presidency then turned their attention to extensive research on Rock Creek Hollow to determine exactly what had happened in that place and to learn the names and stories of the pioneers who were said to have been buried there. Their search in the Church Archives in Salt Lake City and at the Utah State University Special Collections Library in Logan, Utah, confirmed what the Spirit had originally whispered—that Rock Creek Hollow was the scene of some of the most profound and inspiring acts of sacrifice and courage on the Mormon Trail. They were able to identify fifteen who were buried there: thirteen in a common grave, and two men buried separately a few hours later. (Two additional men who died October 25 were identified some time later.) The fifteen who died on October 23–24, 1856, included:

Nils (or Niels) Anderson, age forty-one, from Copenhagen, Denmark. He was a farmer. Nils often carried his fourteen-year-old daughter, Anna, in his handcart.

Elizabeth Haywood Jones Bailey, age fifty-two, from Leigh, Worcestershire, England. She was traveling with her husband and two children. Her husband died later, a few days before entering the Salt Lake Valley.

Samuel Gadd, age ten, from Orwell, Cambridgeshire, England. He was pre-

PATIENCE LOADER ROZSA ARCHER

Patience Loader, a member of the Martin handcart company, recorded this description of an English family in her company in late October:

"I remember well poor Brother Blair. He was a fine, tall man, had been one of Queen Victoria's life guards in London. He had a wife and four children. He made a cover for his cart and put his four children on the cart. He pulled his cart alone, his wife helped by pushing behind. The poor man was so weak and worn down that he fell several times that day but still he kept his dear little children on the cart all day. This man had so much love for his wife and children that instead of eating his morsel of food himself he would give it to his children. Poor man, he pulled the cart as long as he could, then he died and his wife and children had to do the best they could without his help. The children got frozen. Some parts of their bodies were all sores, but they got to Salt Lake City alive."

"Diary of Patience Loader Rosa [Rozsa] Archer." Typescript, Harold B. Lee Library, Brigham Young University, Provo, Utah.

JOSIAH ROGERSON SR.

"Aaron Jackson . . . was found so weak and exhausted when he came to the crossing of the Platte, October 19, that he could not make it, and after he was carried across the ford in a wagon [I] was detailed to wheel the dying Aaron on an empty cart, with his feet dangling over the end bar, to camp.

"After putting up his tent, I assisted his wife [Elizabeth] in laying him in his blankets. It was one of the bitter cold, black, frost nights, . . . and notwithstanding the hard journey the day before, I was awakened at midnight to go on guard again till 6 or 7 in the morning. . . . Passing out through the middle of the tent, my feet struck those of poor Aaron. They were stiff and rebounded at my accidental stumbling. Reaching my hand to his face, I found that he was dead, with his exhausted wife and little ones by his side, all sound asleep. . . .

"Returning to my tent from the night's guarding, I found there one of the most touching pictures of grief and bereavement in the annals of our journey. Mrs. Jackson, apparently just awakened from her slumber, was sitting by the side of her dead husband. Her face was suffused in tears, and between her burst of grief and wails of sorrow, she would wring her hands and tear her hair. Her children blended their cries of 'Father' with that of the mother. This was love, this was affection, grief of the heart, and bereavement of the soul, the like of which I have never seen since."

Salt Lake Tribune, January 14, 1914.

ceded in death by his father and younger brother, who also died along the Mormon Trail.

James Gibb, age sixty-seven, a sailor from Scotland. His wife, Mary, was one of the first converts to the Church from that country. They left their children in Scotland and went ahead to prepare a place for them in the Salt Lake Valley. James was buried in Rock Creek on his wife's fifty-third birthday.

Chesterton John Gillman, listed variously as age forty-seven, sixty-four, or sixty-six, from England. He was a coal miner and a sailor, and the father of eleven children. His wife died in 1854 and, against the wishes of all his children, he made the decision to come to the Salt Lake Valley.

Thomas Girdlestone (or Gurdlestone), age sixty-two, from Norfolk, England. He was the overseer of a large farm and the father of eleven children. His wife died five days later, leaving his twenty-one-year-old daughter, Emma, alone in the company.

William Groves, age twenty-two, a laborer from England. He helped dig the grave for the thirteen who died October 23, and then he and Thomas Girdlestone died and were buried separately the next day.

William James, age forty-six, from Pershore, Worcestershire, England. He was a farm laborer but not robust. His death at Rock Creek left his wife and seven young children without a husband and father.

James Kirkwood, age eleven, from Glasgow, Scotland. He traveled with his widowed mother, Margaret, age forty-seven, and three brothers, Robert, age twenty-one; Thomas, nineteen; and Joseph, four. James's mother had to pull Thomas in the handcart because he was crippled. James carried his youngest brother, Joseph, on his back over snow-covered Rocky Ridge in blizzard conditions. Upon arriving at Rock

Creek Hollow, James set his brother down by the fire, then lay down and died from exhaustion.

Ole Madsen, age forty-one, from Seeland, Denmark. He was a farm laborer. He left behind his wife and four children.

Bodil Mortensen, age ten, from Denmark. She was traveling to be with her sister Margaret, who was already in the Salt Lake Valley. Bodil's parents came to the Salt Lake Valley a year later in 1857 and apparently didn't learn of her death until arriving in Utah.

Niels Mortensen, father of Bodil. Photograph courtesy Marlene Mortensen Burton.

Ella Nielson, age twenty-two, from Jutland, Denmark. She was called "Helle" or Lolly. She was traveling with the Wickland family. Exhausted one day, she was wrapped in a buffalo robe to rest on the trail. Brother Wickland returned later and carried her back to Rock Creek. He had his daughter Christina sleep next to Helle to keep her warm, but to no avail. After she died, her hair had to be clipped from the ice beneath her frozen body.

Niels Nielsen, died five days short of his sixth birthday, from Lolland, Denmark. His father Jens's feet were frozen so badly that he had to be pulled by Sister Nielsen in their handcart. The children struggled in snow that was sometimes knee-deep, suffering greatly from exhaustion and exposure.

Anne Olsen, age forty-six, from Seeland, Denmark. She was from the same branch of the Church as Nils Anderson, who also died at Rock Creek.

Lars Wandelin (or Vendin), age sixty, from Gefle, Sweden. He was a watchmaker who joined the Church in Denmark. He did not want to be buried with his treasured silver watch, so it was turned over to the Perpetual Emigration Fund to assist others in coming to the Salt Lake Valley.

JOSEPH ELDER

"Many can never forget the scenes they witnessed that day [October 21, 1856]. Men, women and children, weakened down by cold and hunger, weeping, crying, and some even dying by the roadside. . . . Oh, how my heart did quake and shudder at the awful scenes which surrounded me."

Joseph Benson Elder, Diaries. Utah State Historical Society, Salt Lake City, Utah.

One member of the Willie company who survived described the common grave at Rock Creek Hollow: "They were laid away in the clothes they wore, in a circle with feet to center and heads out. We covered them with willows and then earth and slid rocks down the hill to keep the wolves from disturbing them. Two of the men who helped dig the grave died and were buried in another nearby." (Robert Reeder, Autobiography. Typescript, Daughters of Utah Pioneers Museum, Salt Lake City, Utah.)

Two more men died on October 25, the day the Willie company left Rock Creek Hollow to press on to the Salt Lake Valley: John Walters, age sixty-four, from Bristol, Somerset, England, and William Smith, age forty-eight, from England, whose wife, Eliza, had died a few days earlier near the Sweetwater River.

The sacred feelings President Lorimer had for Rock Creek Hollow persisted and became more urgent. And yet, there was still some question about what those promptings meant. What needed to be done?

Seeking an answer to that question, President Lorimer took two members of the Riverton Wyoming Stake high council, Mel Baldwin and Phil Huff, to Rock Creek Hollow one evening in September 1989. The place where they knelt in prayer was the site of the common grave. President Lorimer recorded:

"We sought the Lord in prayer, asking that we might understand the significance of the feelings I had been having concerning the site. For some reason I just could not let go of Rock Creek Hollow. A very spiritual event happened that I will never forget. I did not receive an answer, but rather an understanding that I was on the right track and that I was to continue." (Lorimer Journal, pp. 4–5.)

By spiritual confirmation, President Lorimer understood that he was to continue to seek the meaning of the Willie Project. The next step—ultimately the central focus of the project—would soon become clear.

CHAPTER 4

THE TECHNOLOGY

"We felt a sense of urgency to obtain two new computer systems."
PRESIDENT KIM W. McKINNON

THE EVENTS THAT WOULD FINALLY DEFINE THE Willie Project were set in motion by a casual conversation in Lander, Wyoming, in February of 1991. John Kitchen and Kim McKinnon, counselors in the Riverton Wyoming Stake presidency, were in Lander conducting a ward conference along with President Scott Lorimer. While walking down the hall between meetings, the two counselors met Martell Gee from Salt Lake City, who was visiting his brother, former Riverton Wyoming Stake President Lawrence Gee.

They asked Martell what he did for a living, and he told them he worked in the Church's Information Systems Department. The two members of the stake presidency were interested in knowing more. Martell told them of a new computer program the Church was developing to put family history information in CD-ROM format. The new format was wonderfully efficient and saved a tremendous amount of disk space. President Kitchen, who had responsibility over the two family history centers within the stake, asked how their members could become involved in the project. "You can't," replied Martell. "They are only doing it experimentally for now."

This conversation caused President McKinnon to reflect back on an address he had heard four months earlier at the October 1990 general conference of the Church. Elder Richard G. Scott, a member of the Quorum of the Twelve Apostles, had described new advances in computer technology that would dramatically speed the process of researching one's roots and obtaining clearance to perform temple ordinances in behalf of deceased relatives.

"Modern technology has greatly simplified the prior complex rules and regulations for this work," said Elder Scott. "Many brilliant minds and sensitive hearts have harnessed advanced technology to provide personal computer helps. . . . FamilySearch provides members easy access to the Church's central genealogy computer files. It greatly simplifies research and enables members to more efficiently find information in the Church's vast storehouse of microfilmed records. The computer provides direct, rapid search of a large compilation of valuable information on compact disks without time or error of searching traditional microfilm or microfiche." (*Ensign,* November 1990, p. 6.)

After the conversation with Martell Gee, and remembering what Elder Scott had said, President McKinnon suddenly felt it was essential to get these computer systems for the two family history centers in the Riverton stake. The feeling of urgency was sudden and unexplained, much like President Lorimer's feelings concerning Rock Creek Hollow and the Willie Project. At this time, however, there were only six computer systems in the Church using the newly developed family history software. They were not yet readily available to the general Church membership. Still, the Riverton Wyoming Stake wanted two of those computers. To most it seemed impossible.

President McKinnon was not new to the world of computers. After graduating from the University of Idaho at Moscow, he had taught computer courses, and he had a keen interest in technology. He would later express his conviction that his training and interest in computers was the Lord's way of preparing him for the role he would play in the Willie Project.

The sense of urgency would not leave President McKinnon. He received permission from President Lorimer to try to obtain computers for the stake's family history libraries. Soon after that, while he was in Salt Lake City attending some business meetings, President McKinnon walked over to the Church's Family History Library and inquired as to whether the Riverton stake could get on a waiting list to receive the computer equipment and software. A man took down his name and address, but nothing happened. Weeks turned into months with no word from Salt Lake City.

Telephone calls placed by Dianne Tippets, the Riverton stake family history librarian, to the Church Purchasing Division proved discouraging. It appeared the stake had been talking to the wrong people all along. President McKinnon again felt compelled beyond his own will. He took a day off work and drove to Church headquarters in Salt Lake City, a six-hour trip one way. After persuasively communicating his sense of urgency in the matter to Alan Reddish of the Purchasing Department, he filled out request forms and was promised some results. Among President McKinnon's last words to Alan as he left his office were, "We really need these computers!" Two weeks later, on April 24, 1991, two computers, two printers, and two full sets of family history CDs arrived in Riverton.

Family History Library, Salt Lake City, Utah

With great excitement and humility, the stake presidency set up one computer system in the family history library at the Riverton stake center and placed the other in a similar facility in Lander, Wyoming. The stake members were told that they now had the only family history computer systems operating outside of Utah's Wasatch Front.

Later that same evening, President Lorimer and President McKinnon were driving to the Wind River Branch in Fort Washakie to conduct some routine Church business. President McKinnon was reflecting on the sense of urgency he had felt concerning the acquisition of the new systems. He wondered aloud to President Lorimer: "Why have I felt so pushed about obtaining these computers? Why the great sense of urgency? Why did I feel so compelled to go to Salt Lake City?"

President Lorimer's response would surprise both of them. After a long pause, he turned to his counselor and blurted out, "It's the Willie people!"

Donna Olsen of the Riverton Wyoming Stake at the computer.

"What?" asked a very surprised President McKinnon. "What made you think of them?"

President Lorimer replied: "That's why we have the computers. Their temple work has not been done."

President Lorimer would later say that the words had come into his mind in a distinct and unconfused manner, in a way that he had never before experienced. They seemed to be placed in his mouth from an outside source. He and President McKinnon looked at each other in disbelief. Thoughts came fast: *This can't be. Surely temple work has been done for these courageous pioneers, many of whom gave their lives for their testimonies of the restored gospel. Surely their descendants have taken care of it.* Despite these doubts, the feeling remained: Temple work for the Willie and Martin people needed to be completed.

Business finished in the Wind River Branch, President Lorimer and President McKinnon could hardly wait to get back to the new computer at the stake center in Riverton to look up temple ordinance data for some of the handcart pioneers. They started with the fifteen members of the James G. Willie company who died October 23–24, 1856, and were buried at Rock Creek Hollow. The first name they searched on the computer was that of eleven-year-old James Kirkwood. They were hard-pressed to control their emotions as they discovered that James was still waiting to be sealed to his parents through the power of the holy Melchizedek Priesthood.

Bodil Mortensen, the ten-year-old girl who died after climbing over

Rocky Ridge into Rock Creek Hollow, was also waiting for her temple ordinances to be completed. There was no evidence that she had even been baptized yet.

Name after name appeared on the computer screen showing missing ordinances. In all, for those fifteen handcart pioneers buried at Rock Creek Hollow, 82 percent of the temple ordinances had not yet been completed. These people had accepted the gospel and were heeding the prophet's call to gather with the rest of the Latter-day Saints in Salt Lake City, but their journey ended too soon.

With prayerful, hopeful hearts, the Riverton stake presidency applied for official approval from their Regional Representative, Area President, and a member of the First Presidency to submit these names for temple work. Because of the special circumstances surrounding the project and the inspired feelings of those involved, permission was granted by the appropriate priesthood leaders. The research was confirmed with the International Genealogical Index (IGI), and information was then submitted manually to the Church. The Family History Department soon confirmed that the research was accurate, and clearance was granted for temple ordinances to be performed.

The question was now being asked, "Why now and why us?" Church officials in Salt Lake City suggested that this project would not have been possible until the computer resources were developed to allow it to happen. Furthermore, the handcart pioneers died within the confines of the Riverton Wyoming Stake, and President Lorimer was, in a manner of speaking, their stake president. Now that the time was right, it was appropriate that the inspiration for this work should come to him.

The stake presidency now felt sure that the fifteen individuals buried at Rock Creek Hollow represented hundreds of others who were also waiting for their temple ordinances. Many of the pioneers who died on the Mormon Trail left no descendants and therefore had no family members searching for their names. Many who died before reaching the Salt Lake Valley had truly become lost souls out on the prairie.

The rescue effort initiated by Brigham Young in October of 1856 brought the surviving pioneers safely to the Salt Lake Valley. Now, a "Second Rescue" was needed to provide the sacred ordinances of the temple for those faithful pioneers. With the clearing of temple ordinances for those buried at Rock Creek Hollow, the Second Rescue of the Willie and Martin handcart pioneers, a very sacred and spiritual rescue, was just beginning.

CHAPTER 5

HELP FROM THE OGDEN TEMPLE

"We stand ready to receive you."

OGDEN TEMPLE PRESIDENT DORMAN H. BAIRD

WHEN DORMAN H. BAIRD WAS CALLED ON September 1, 1990, to serve as president of the Ogden Temple in Utah, he knew something of the rich, spiritual experiences associated with temple service. He did not know at the time, however, that the new presidency and the temple recorder would play a central role in performing thousands of temple ordinances for the Willie and Martin handcart pioneers.

The Second Rescue of those devoted pioneers centered on temple ordinances. It therefore required a sacred temple setting, a dedicated temple presidency, willing officiators, and the promptings of the Spirit. Step by step, those promptings led to the doors of the Ogden Temple.

President Baird first met Riverton Wyoming Stake President Scott Lorimer on May 18, 1991. The Ogden Temple presidency were traveling to various locations within their temple district and meeting with stake presidencies, hoping to encourage and foster increased temple attendance. President Baird and his second counselor, Dale Gardner, held such a meeting in Evanston for the Wyoming stake presidencies.

After the meeting, President Lorimer introduced himself to President Baird. He said, "If you've got some time, my counselors and I need to talk to you. We've had some very special experiences relative to the Willie and Martin handcart people. We feel we have a great responsibility to help provide temple work for these people who died on the plains of Wyoming." President Baird was immediately interested. He later recalled that the conversation was "a very moving experience."

Two weeks later, on June 7, 1991, the Riverton stake presidency traveled to Salt Lake City. Armed with carefully compiled maps, overlays, and booklets detailing their experiences thus far, the presidency hoped to convince Church leaders to purchase land in Wyoming that included sites important to the tragic and heroic handcart journeys.

Although they lived within the boundaries of the Ogden Utah Temple district, the Riverton stake presidency explored the possibility of performing the ordinances for the Willie and Martin pioneers in the Salt Lake Temple, considered by some to be the "pioneer temple." The stake presidency met briefly with Dave Wright, the Salt Lake Temple recorder.

Afterward, over a bowl of soup at a nearby restaurant, the Riverton stake presidency decided to make one more stop before driving home to Wyoming. They drove to meet with the Ogden Temple presidency concerning the Second Rescue.

It turned out to be the right thing to do. President Lorimer recalled: "One of the underlying principles of the Second Rescue project was obedience. Even though the names for [those who died at Rock Creek Hollow] had been submitted to the Salt Lake Temple and were ready for processing, it was decided it would be better to be obedient and go to our assigned temple in Ogden. What a tragedy it would have been if the work would have been done anywhere else. In the Ogden Temple there were workers, a recorder, and a presidency that had been prepared to complete the spiritual portion of the Second Rescue. Everyone was blessed because of obedience." (Lorimer Personal Writings, "Stories," number 5.)

Although President Baird was not available when they arrived in Ogden, the stake presidency members were warmly received by Artwell B. Checketts, first counselor in the Ogden Temple presidency, and Robert Memmott, the temple recorder. As they sat in a private temple room and shared their sacred experiences concerning the handcart pioneers, the Spirit took charge.

President Checketts and Brother Memmott knew immediately that this was no ordinary request or project. They sensed the magnitude and spiritual significance of the assignment, and they humbly extended an invitation for the Riverton Latter-day Saints to accomplish the work at the Ogden Temple. The invitation was accepted.

Brother Memmott, the temple recorder, would play a particularly important role in the Second Rescue project. He was well prepared for the task, having worked in the Church's Family History Department for nine years and served as assistant recorder at the Salt Lake Temple for two. He was thus well acquainted with research and temple clearance procedures. When President Lorimer showed Brother Memmott a chart listing those who had died at Rock Creek Hollow and the high number of missing ordinances, Brother Memmott asked with focused emotion: "What can we do to help?"

Robert Memmott,
Ogden Temple recorder

There were many details to work out. Research showed that less than 20 percent of all possible temple ordinances had been completed for the fifteen who had died at Rock Creek Hollow. They realized this might be only the tip of the iceberg. There could be hundreds if not thousands of ordinances waiting to be completed for other members of those pioneer companies. A separate and very large file of handcart pioneer names would need to be created.

After the research was completed and the names were cleared for ordinance work, a way needed to be found to make sure Riverton stake members could personally do the temple work for those whose names they had researched. Brother Memmott immediately began drawing up plans for how this could all be done efficiently and in an orderly manner. President Lorimer and his counselors left that meeting feeling confident that the Ogden Temple was the place the Lord intended for them to accomplish the sacred ordinances for the Willie and Martin handcart pioneers.

Reflecting on this and other meetings they had attended that day, President Lorimer recorded in his journal for June 7, 1991, "The day was one of the most perfect of my entire life." The Riverton stake presidency had had several successful conversations with Church leaders who would play key roles in furthering the two goals of the Second Rescue: the completion of the temple work for the handcart pioneers, and the eventual acquisition of land sites important to the handcart stories. President Gordon B. Hinckley, at that time First Counselor in the First Presidency of the Church, was especially supportive. The long hours of prayer, travel, research, writing, and map drawing were bearing fruit in a remarkable way.

The next challenge was to bear testimony of the Second Rescue to the members of the Riverton Wyoming Stake and enlist their support for the monumental project that now lay ahead.

CHAPTER 6

RIVERTON WYOMING STAKE MEETING

"Brethren and sisters, we have been called to do a great work."
PRESIDENT R. SCOTT LORIMER

THE SECOND RESCUE WAS INDEED AN enormous project. The names of more than a thousand pioneers needed to be researched to verify dates and localities and to establish family ties. Then the actual temple ordinances needed to be completed in the Ogden Temple, more than 300 miles away.

President Lorimer and his two counselors could see great spiritual benefits in involving as many people as possible in the work. What was the best way to testify of the spiritual influences that had led them this far? What was the best way to convince stake members of the importance of the project in their own lives and the lives of their families?

After consulting with the members of the stake high council, the stake presidency decided to hold a special stake meeting. President Lorimer later commented, "I knew that this assignment we had received to do temple work for the handcart pioneers was a lot bigger than any of us would ever dream, and it was . . . a very spiritual thing. It needed to be presented in a very spiritual way." (Lorimer Oral History, p. 14.)

At the meeting, which was held Sunday, July 21, 1991, the members of the stake presidency explained to the congregation the origins and importance of the great and sacred project now referred to as the "Second Rescue." They asked the members to make a sincere and full commitment to participate. President Lorimer stirred the hearts of the Riverton Saints by comparing the Second Rescue to the first rescue of 1856:

"The similarities of this Second Rescue to the first are numerous. President Brigham Young spoke in Salt Lake . . . concerning the urgency of rescuing the pioneers who were stranded on the plains of Wyoming.

BRIGHAM YOUNG

Upon hearing that more than a thousand pioneers were still hundreds of miles away from Salt Lake in snowy, winter weather, President Brigham Young made a plea for help from the Saints in the Valley during general conference, October 5, 1856:

"I shall call upon the Bishops this day. I shall not wait until tomorrow, nor until the next day, for 60 good mule teams and 12 or 15 wagons. I do not want to send oxen. I want good horses and mules. They are in this Territory and we must have them. Also 12 tons of flour and 40 good teamsters, besides those that drive the teams."

Reported in *Deseret News*, October 15, 1856.

He didn't mince any words; he encouraged the people to go. He promised them that if they did not, the Lord would curse their surpluses with mildew. I thought that was interesting. We're not going to promise you that. He also was frustrated that it didn't go fast enough. You will see and hear the stake presidency . . . and the high council asking [from time to time] how the Second Rescue is going.

"President Brigham Young called upon the bishops of the Church to supply the needs of the Willie and the Martin handcart companies. He requested very specific things. He asked them to bring strong animals, good wagons, and flour and beef stock to feed the pioneers. Many of the rescuers became discouraged and were willing to turn back prior to reaching Fort Bridger. Comments in their journals say they felt that no man or woman could survive the terrible storm that was brewing on South Pass. Later, the pioneers gave great thanks to those brethren who were willing to go ahead and risk all that they had.

"The first rescue wasn't convenient. . . . The Saints in the Salt Lake Valley had been plagued once again with the problem of locusts. . . . When Brigham Young stood in the Tabernacle and asked for all those teams and wagons, the Saints had not even harvested their crops, what was left of them. They had not gotten their wood in for the winter, and Brigham Young was very fearful that the Saints once again would be deprived of the bare necessities of life in the Salt Lake Valley. He personally . . . committed an enormous amount of money—$60,000—to bring the Saints in from the high plains of Wyoming. It was not convenient at all, what those Saints did for their brethren and sisters in the gospel. They went out willingly, however, and saved those people.

"Today I call upon the bishops of this stake, and I leave it in their hands how this rescue will unfold. I know that the Spirit will rest upon them. I urge you, brethren, to make sure nothing goes undone. I promise you that we will succeed in what we've been asked to do." (Meetings of the Second Rescue.)

Presidents Kitchen and McKinnon, counselors in the stake presidency, told the stake members remarkable stories of the handcart pioneers and their rescuers who were still waiting for their temple work to be done. President Kitchen paid special tribute to the rescuers who responded so quickly and so courageously to Brigham Young's call for help:

"One of those, Ephraim Hanks, was considered to be one of the best scouts in the Utah territory. In early October of 1856, he was on a fishing expedition at Utah Lake. One night, he had a dream. He was visited by 'an ordinary sized' man who appeared to him and said that there were handcart companies on the plains and they needed his help. Hanks immediately left his fishing expedition and went home and prepared for his duty of going and helping. When he arrived in Salt Lake City, general conference was just beginning and the prophet Brigham Young had just received news of the belated handcart companies on the plains. He was concerned about their safety and was in the process of organizing the first rescue of those people." (Meetings of the Second Rescue.) Ephraim Hanks volunteered to go at once and was on his way the next morning, alone, driving a light wagon.

In his talk, President McKinnon reviewed the story of little Bodil Mortensen and explained how and why she had come to symbolize the importance of the Second Rescue: "Our research discovered that Bodil, who was nine at the time she left Denmark, traveled with the Jens Nielsen family to get to Salt Lake City where her older sister was. She was not a member of the Peter Mortensen family. She did not have any descendants to research her line. She is not even listed on the roster of the Willie handcart company. She was a forgotten little soul all alone in a foreign land, perhaps not understanding the language and what was going on, caught in a terrible snowstorm. She has waited 135 years for all of this to come together, 135 years to . . . finally join the Church, to finally receive the blessings of temple ordinances.

"Brothers and sisters, can you begin to understand why this has been so important for President Lorimer? Can you begin to understand why he's

Ephraim K. Hanks

EPHRAIM K. HANKS

One of the rescuers from the Salt Lake Valley reported how he found the Martin Company at last:

"I think the sun was about an hour high in the west when I spied something in the distance that looked like a black streak in the snow. As I got near to it, I perceived it moved; then I was satisfied that this was the long looked for handcart company led by Captain Edward Martin."

Andrew Jenson, "The Belated Emigration of 1856," *Contributor* 14 (January 1893): 203. Photograph courtesy Archives, the Historical Department of The Church of Jesus Christ of Latter-day Saints.

WILLIAM WOODWARD

"A number of years after the handcart trek, William Woodward was at a general conference in Salt Lake. He met a woman who had been one of his Hundred [in the Willie company]. She reminded him of some good rawhide shoes which were owned by one of the men in the party. William did remember them, and she then asked if he ever wondered what had happened to them. [Evidently they turned up missing one day.] The woman told William that she had taken them one night and made soup with them."

Told by Cecil Woodward, William's son, as printed in *History of William Woodward, 1833–1908,* typescript in possession of Daina Zollinger, River Heights, Utah.

asked us to pray so that we would know the importance of this work? Can you begin to catch the vision of why our Heavenly Father has called him at this time both to serve and to lead us? Can you begin to feel the spirit of this people and the promptings we have received? I testify to you that the Willie people are watching over this stake with great interest. They have influenced many, and they will influence many more. . . . I promise you and I promise the Willie people that before stake conference, Bodil Mortensen and the others who died and are buried at Rock Creek will have their temple ordinances completed in the House of the Lord." (Meetings of the Second Rescue.)

Near the end of the meeting, the stake presidency handed out to the bishops and branch presidents packets containing names of Willie and Martin handcart pioneers as well as their rescuers. President Lorimer then advised: "The bishops are to kneel in prayer with their correlation councils and assign those names to the members of this stake. There is a name for every member of our stake who is active and over the age of twelve. . . . The youth are to participate in this project, . . . the elders quorum presidents, . . . and the high priest group leaders. . . . Their responsibility is to share the load of the bishop . . . and to see that the work is done. We cannot stop until it is completed. . . .

"Brethren and sisters, we have been called to do a great work. . . . This stake will be changed. Our lives will be changed because of what we are going to do. . . . The story of the Willie and the Martin handcart pioneers and their rescue is a story of commitment to the gospel and of an understanding of the importance of the principles of salvation. . . . Start looking at your own [ancestors], because in your family, there are hundreds of Bodil Mortensens who need their work done. . . . When you become discouraged, kneel down and ask for help. These people will provide it. They will be there to assist you.

"These people have been here this day. The spirit that you have felt has been theirs. They beg you and ask you to be faithful. Don't turn back before you get to Fort Bridger. Get the work done." (Meetings of the Second Rescue.)

The Riverton stake members responded humbly, enthusiastically, and with real commitment. One member, Evelyn Irene, testified: "When we were first called to the special stake meeting where we learned about the Second Rescue, I felt an urgency and need as I listened. Could we have seen beyond the veil, the chapel aisles would have been filled with those anxiously waiting for their work to be done. The spirit we felt in [that] meeting—I know they were there! There had to be a great rejoicing going on! We have felt that joy and the help as the work went speedily forward. There was an excitement as everyone researched the names." (Riverton Stake Member Journals, p. 167.)

President Lorimer concluded the meeting with a resounding call for commitment: "When I used to go to Rock Creek Hollow, I would get a sad feeling. Today is a great day. Today those people buried at Rock Creek Hollow are beginning the final end of their earthly trip and of their experience as Mormon pioneers. They will receive their eternal blessings, the rewards which have been promised for faithful service in the kingdom.

"Do not become discouraged. . . . This project will change your lives. It has changed mine. I'm grateful to have been a small part of it." (Meetings of the Second Rescue.)

The date of the special stake meeting, Sunday, July 21, 1991, remains sacred and historic for many people. Lives of the living and the dead were beginning to change, and the Second Rescue of the Willie and Martin handcart pioneers was officially organized, under the direction of the restored priesthood.

ELIZABETH JACKSON

"We camped out with nothing but the vault of Heaven for a roof, and the stars for companions. The snow lay several inches deep upon the ground. The night was bitterly cold. I sat down on a rock with one child in my lap and one on each side of me. In that condition I remained until morning.

" . . . It will be readily perceived that under such adverse circumstances I had become despondent. I was six or seven thousand miles from my native land in wild, rocky mountain country, in a destitute condition, the ground covered with snow, the waters covered with ice, and I with three fatherless children with scarcely nothing to protect them from the merciless storms.

"When I retired to bed that night, being the 27th of Oct., I had a stunning revelation. In my dream my husband stood by me and said—'Cheer up, Elizabeth, deliverance is at hand.'"

The next day, October 28, the express team of rescuers from the Salt Lake Valley found them.

Elizabeth Kingsford, *Leaves from the Life of Elizabeth Horrocks Jackson Kingsford*. Ogden, Utah, 1908.

CHAPTER 7

THE TEMPLE WORK BEGINS

"These people are certainly accepting what we are doing here today."
OGDEN TEMPLE PRESIDENT DORMAN H. BAIRD

LESS THAN A MONTH AFTER THE STAKE SECOND Rescue meeting, the first sacred ordinances were completed in the Ogden Temple for some of the 1856 handcart pioneers. On August 14, 1991, the Riverton stake presidency, stake patriarch, members of the high council, and their families began the next phase of the Second Rescue. On that memorable day, temple work was completed for members of the Willie handcart company who died in Rock Creek Hollow on October 23–24, 1856, as well as some of the pioneers' family members.

Ogden Temple President Dorman Baird spoke solemnly of that day in the temple: "That was a day I'll never forget. We first met in the baptistry. The stake presidency and some of their children had come to do baptisms. There was a lovely spirit present. It was hard for me to keep my composure even while greeting them and welcoming them. We commenced by taking the children into the waters of baptism. What a great experience! The adults went on and did the [other ordinances].

"Later, after lunch, we met in the sealing room. We commenced with the names [of those who died at] Rock Creek Hollow. I had done very little sealing for the dead at that time. Robert Memmott, the temple recorder, was a witness. There was such a strong, spiritual feeling. Many times I just had to stop. I just couldn't get through it. When we were through I told the group that several of these deceased people had been there that day and they were very pleased with what we were doing." (Baird Taped Interview.)

For Riverton stake members attending the temple that day as families, it was an especially emotional time. Diane McKinnon, wife of President Kim McKinnon, wrote: "August 14, 1991, was a very special and sacred day for our family. We were at the Ogden Temple by 6:30 A.M. The children of the stake presidency got to [enter the font to] do the baptisms, and the fathers of the children performed the baptisms. There were some remaining names so President Lorimer, President Kitchen, and [my husband] Kim baptized each other. What a wonderful thing that was to see them clothed in white, baptizing one another in behalf of the departed handcart pioneers.

Riverton Wyoming Stake presidency with Ogden Temple president. Left to right: John L. Kitchen, Jr., President R. Scott Lorimer, President Dorman H. Baird, Kim W. McKinnon.

"After the baptisms, I was given the honor of performing sacred temple work for little Bodil Mortensen. She is the [ten-year-old girl whose name] I found in the Church Archive records when Kim and I went [to Salt Lake City] in March of 1990. It was her story that so impressed both me and Kim that day. Her temple work had never been done. I can't begin to write about how humbled I was at being able to be the one to do her work. What a special privilege that was! I felt her spirit strongly as I did her work. . . . We all went through an endowment session together. President and Sister Lorimer were the witnesses. As we entered the celestial room, we just hugged each other and cried over the special experiences we had witnessed. I felt so close to Heavenly Father, Jesus, Bodil, and especially my dear husband, Kim." (Diane Isom McKinnon Personal Journal.)

Before they left the temple that afternoon, President Baird invited the entire Wyoming group to have dinner in the President's dining room. After the meal, he told them that he had never before felt such a strong spirit in the temple as he had that day. President Baird thanked them for allowing

JOHN CHISLETT

"I was installed as regular commissary to the camp. The brethren turned over to me flour, potatoes, onions, and a limited supply of warm clothing for both sexes, besides quilts, blankets, buffalo robes, woollen socks, etc. I first distributed the necessary provisions, and after supper divided the clothing, bedding, etc., where it was most needed. That evening, for the first time in quite a period, the songs of Zion were to be heard in the camp, and peals of laughter issued from the little knots of people as they chatted around the fires. The change seemed almost miraculous, so sudden was it from grave to gay, from sorrow to gladness, from mourning to rejoicing. With the cravings of hunger satisfied, and with hearts filled with gratitude to God and our good brethren, we all united in prayer, and then retired to rest."

John Chislett narrative published in T.B.H. Stenhouse, *The Rocky Mountain Saints*. New York: D. Appleton, 1873.

him and the Ogden Temple workers to participate in doing temple work for these "precious names."

On the return trip home to Wyoming from Ogden, President Lorimer and his family could not resist stopping at Rock Creek Hollow to contemplate the events of the day. With the temple work now completed for those whose bodies lay there in the mass grave, the Lorimer family noticed a new spirit in the Hollow. President Lorimer wrote: "No longer was there a feeling of suffering, rather a feeling of joy. The work was now completed for these faithful people and they could progress . . . . I was grateful to them all, especially Bodil, as she had been such an influence in my life. I gathered a small bouquet of flowers and placed them beside her name on the headstone at the mass grave. That day I left a better man for having had the opportunity of getting to meet these faithful people."

Accomplishing temple work for those who died at Rock Creek Hollow was only the beginning. Soon, hundreds of Riverton Wyoming Stake members would come to the Ogden Temple to participate in ordinances for the handcart pioneers they had searched out and learned to love.

CHAPTER 8

A YEAR OF RICH SPIRITUAL EXPERIENCES

"Family history research here went completely out of sight.
The things that were found were just tremendous."

PRESIDENT JOHN L. KITCHEN, JR.

By JULY 21, 1991, AT THE CONCLUSION OF THE special Second Rescue meeting, the stage was set in the Riverton Wyoming Stake for an outpouring of remarkable spiritual experiences. Bishops and branch presidents gave the name of a Willie or Martin handcart pioneer or a rescuer to each member of the stake interested in participating. People twelve years of age and older contributed to the effort.

The assignment was not an easy one. First, most would need to receive instruction on how to use the new computers and programs in the family history libraries in Lander and Riverton. Second, they would use that training to check for the correct spelling of the names, locate birth, marriage, and death dates, and construct family relationships by identifying names of the pioneers' parents, children, and spouses. Finally, stake members would search for evidence of temple ordinances already completed. If any ordinances still needed to be performed for a person, the stake member would then submit the name and accompanying information to be approved for temple work. When the name was cleared, the person doing the research was responsible to complete the temple work in Ogden, Utah, or to ask someone else to perform the ordinances.

If the stake presidency had any doubts about the response of stake members to the project, those doubts were quickly dispelled. Not only did active members of the Church participate, but it is estimated that 20 to 25 percent of the more than 1100 names were researched by less-active members.

EPHRAIM K. HANKS

"The sight that met my gaze as I entered their [handcart] camp, can never be erased from my memory. The starved forms and haggard countenances of the poor sufferers as they moved about slowly, shivering with cold, to prepare their scanty evening meal, was enough to touch the stoutest heart. When they saw me coming, they hailed me with joy inexpressible, and when they further beheld the supply of fresh [buffalo] meat I brought into their camp, their gratitude knew no bounds. Flocking around me, one would say, "Oh please, give me a small piece of meat," another would exclaim, "My poor children are starving, do give me a little," and children with tears in their eyes would call out, "Give me some, give me some." At first, I tried to wait on them, and handed out the meat as they called for it, but finally I told them to help themselves. Five minutes later, both my horses had been released of their extra burden, the meat was all gone, and the next few hours found the people in camp busily engaged cooking and eating it with thankful hearts."

Andrew Jenson, "The Belated Emigration of 1856," *Contributor* 14 (January 1893): 203.

President John Kitchen, counselor to President Lorimer, described the enthusiasm for the project: "Family history research here went completely out of sight. We [used to have] family history centers open [about] three hours a week. [Now] they were [of necessity] open from six in the morning until ten at night, and it was busy all of that time. The things that were found were just tremendous!

"[For example,] Don and Luann Green in our stake had a [pioneer] family they were researching. They made three or four trips to Salt Lake City just to do research, and that wasn't out of line with what a lot of other people were doing. People would travel twelve hours [round trip] to the Ogden Temple to do one baptism." (Martin's Cove Presentation.)

Gene Duncan of Lander and Dianne Tippets and Donna Olsen of Riverton were primarily responsible for training stake members to use the computers and the FamilySearch® program to do their research. Sister Tippets recalled: "It was at this time that the Family History Center began to breathe new life. . . . It was exciting to see the increased activity in the center and to see individuals search not only for the names assigned to them with the handcart project but [for] their own ancestors. It was also good to see the nonmember librarians spend unselfish hours helping Church members learn how to do genealogical research." (Riverton Wyoming Stake Member Journals, p. 240.)

Librarians found that the youth were among the most enthused and fearless in learning to use the computers. President Lorimer wrote: "Because everyone over the age of twelve was given a name of [a] handcart pioneer, the deacons, teachers, priests, Laurels, Mia Maids, and Beehives were involved in family history research. It was found that the youth were much more adept at running the computers than many of the adults. They had no fear of the new technology. General Authorities and others would marvel as they heard of deacons quorums actually processing names through the TempleReady™ [program] and doing it willingly and correctly. During the Second Rescue, one Laurel of the stake processed thousands of ordinances for temple work during her summer [vacation] to assist the stake presidency." (Lorimer Personal Writings, "Stories," number 4.)

The stake presidency, high council, and many other volunteers gathered lists and data to help with the research. Just the task of organizing the paperwork was enormous. Stake members spent untold hours reading journals and highlighting names, dates, cities, ships, and countries. Individuals checked and rechecked names, doing anything to help locate enough information to make it possible for a pioneer to receive temple ordinances. To ensure that the research data was organized and accessible, more than 90,000 pages of research were paginated and indexed.

Melvin Bashore of the Church Historical Department was of tremendous help in providing information about those who perished along the way to the Salt Lake Valley from the Willie and Martin companies. Although Captain Edward Martin's journal of the trek was unfortunately destroyed, making research for his company much more difficult, Brother Bashore was able to find important information on 96 percent of those who had apparently died in the Willie company and 61 percent in the Martin company. Brother Bashore's research provided information that opened the doors of the temple and its sacred ordinances to many of the pioneer dead.

Originally the Riverton Saints had planned to research only the 1,000-plus names of the Willie and Martin handcart pioneers. However, Elder Hartman Rector, Jr., who at the time was serving as a member of the First Quorum of the Seventy, came to their stake conference in March of 1992 and reiterated the great importance of sealing families together. He strongly urged them to locate parents, brothers and sisters, and children of the pioneers in order to ensure that eternal family ties were made at the

DAN JONES

Dan Jones, one of the rescuers, tells of finding the Martin company a few miles east of Independence Rock:

"A condition of distress here met my eyes that I never saw before or since. The train was strung out for three or four miles. There were old men pulling and tugging their carts, sometimes loaded with a sick wife or children—women pulling along sick husbands—little children six to eight years old struggling through the mud and snow. As night came on the mud would freeze on their clothes and feet. There were two of us, and hundreds needing help. What could we do? We gathered on to some of the most helpless with our ropes tied to the carts, and helped as many as we could into camp. This was a bitter, cold night and we had no fuel except very small sage brush. Several died that night. Next morning we started for our camp near Devil's Gate."

Daniel W. Jones, *Forty Years among the Indians.* Salt Lake City: Juvenile Instructor's Office, 1890, pp. 68–69.

PATIENCE LOADER ROZSA ARCHER

"During the time we was waiting [for supper] a good brother came to our camp fire. . . . He asked Mother if she had no husband. She told [him] her husband had died two months ago and he was buried on the plains. He had been standing with his hands behind him, then he handed us a nice piece of beef to cook for our supper. He left us and came back with a beef bone. He said, 'Here is a bone to make you some soup and don't quarrel over it.' We felt surprised that he should think we would ever quarrel over our food. Mother said, 'Oh brother, we never quarrel over having short rations, but we feel very thankful to you for giving us this meat for we had not got any meat, neither did we expect to have any.'"

"Diary of Patience Loader Rosa [Rozsa] Archer." Typescript, Harold B. Lee Library, Brigham Young University, Provo, Utah, p. 85.

temple. With that plea, the work of the Riverton stake members quadrupled overnight.

During the Second Rescue, demand was great for computer time. In order to give everyone a chance, families were given half-hour turns at the family history centers. It was a common occurrence at the libraries for families to find the information needed to clear a name for temple ordinances. So intense was the interest that for a family member to be absent when such a discovery was made was a real disappointment.

Late one evening in the Riverton family history center, a family had been researching the Hosea Stout family with limited success. By about 10:30 P.M., the seven children had become restless. The mother agreed to take six of the children home and get them ready for bed while the father and an older daughter continued the research.

Minutes after the majority of the family left, the father and daughter finally located the records for the Hosea Stout family on the computer. They hurried home with excitement to tell of their discovery. Everyone was thrilled except one eleven-year-old daughter. She quietly went to her bedroom and called her bishop to ask if there were any more "Willie names," explaining her disappointment that she had not been there when the information on the other names was found. Bishop Gary Anderson explained that he did not have any more female names, but he had one male name, James Alfred Peacock. Heika Lorimer said she would be very pleased to do his research even though she knew she could not be proxy for any of his temple work.

No records of James Alfred Peacock could be found. Heika ordered a microfilm from Salt Lake City to see if she could locate him on census or parish records. She patiently searched the film for hours for James Peacock. Many adults were beginning to doubt whether she would ever find him. She ordered more microfilm and continued reading. Finally, one Sunday afternoon, her disappointment turned to joy. She found a birth record for James Alfred Peacock, saw that his temple work had not been completed, and processed and cleared his name for temple ordinances. Such was the excitement and spirit of service that accompanied the Second Rescue.

Many individuals had personal experiences that confirmed in their minds the importance of the work they were doing. One such person was Mary Hereford, a Lamanite member of the Wind River Branch. In the fall of 1991, Mary was given a paper by her branch president assigning her to research the name of Ephramine Wickland, a one-year-old girl who was a member of the Willie company. Shortly thereafter, the home in which Sister Hereford lived burned to the ground. In the terror of watching the fire, she remembered the paper that had been given to her with the name of the little pioneer girl. She later described her feelings as she stood outside watching her home burn:

"Standing outside . . . I said a little prayer, 'Please Lord, don't let the paper [burn].' When the firemen said we could go in, I looked around and started to cry. The house had been very badly burned and there was a lot of smoke damage. . . . The next day we went back to the house to see if we could save anything. . . . The kitchen was the worst. My microwave was melted to a crisp. While looking on top of the refrigerator I found the [Second Rescue] paper. . . .

"Everything on the paper was burnt except that my name and the person whose work was to be done were white. The names seemed to be highlighted. I was very surprised. I told my [nonmember] husband that I was assigned to research this person and do her temple work. My husband drove me to the library and waited while I did the research. I wanted to know more about the Willie handcart company so I . . . read about it. While reading I also located my husband's great-great-grandma who was adopted by a family. I am very thankful to have had a chance to do the

ANN JEWELL ROWLEY

"There came a time, when there seemed to be no food at all. Some of the men left to hunt buffalo. Night was coming and there was no food for the evening meal. I asked God's help as I always did. I got on my knees, remembering two hard sea biscuits that were still in my trunk. They had been left over from the sea voyage, they were not large, and were so hard, they couldn't be broken. Surely, that was not enough to feed 8 people, but 5 loaves and 2 fishes were not enough to feed 5000 people either, but through a miracle, Jesus had done it. So, with God's help, nothing is impossible. I found the biscuits and put them in a dutch oven and covered them with water and asked for God's blessing, then I put the lid on the pan and set it on the coals. When I took off the lid a little later, I found the pan filled with food. I kneeled with my family and thanked God for his goodness. That night my family had sufficient food. The men returned with buffalo meat, and what wasn't eaten right away by the Saints, was dried into jerky."

Autobiography of Ann Jewell Rowley, in James Albert Jones, *Some Early Pioneers of Huntington, Utah and Surrounding Area,* 1980, pp. 241–47.

JOHN JAQUES

Even after the rescuers came from Salt Lake to assist, the trials were not over:

"The handcart company rested in Martin's Ravine [Cove] two or three or more days. Though under the shelter of the northern mountains, it was a cold place. One night the gusty wind blew over a number of the tents, and it was with difficulty some of the emigrants could keep from freezing.

" . . . By this time there was a sufficiency of wagons to take in most if not all of the baggage of the company, and to carry some of the people. It was a trying time that day in leaving the ravine. One perplexing difficulty was to determine who should ride, for many must still walk . . . and certainly for most of the company, the cart-pulling occupation was gone. There was considerable crying of women and children, and perhaps of a few of the men, whom the wagons could not accommodate with a ride. One of the relief party remarked that in all the mobbings and drivings of the Mormons he had seen nothing like it. C. H. Wheelock could scarcely refrain from shedding tears, and he declared that he would willingly give his own life if that would save the lives of the emigrants."

Stella Jaques Bell, ed., *Life History and Writings of John Jaques, including a Diary of the Martin Handcart Company*. Rexburg, Idaho: Ricks College Press, 1978.

Lord's work." (Riverton Wyoming Stake Member Journals, p. 518.)

Mary Hereford insisted that the only reason the paper did not burn with the rest of her possessions was that Ephramine, the little pioneer girl, wanted her temple work completed. Later, Sister Hereford's research bore out the fact that there was indeed sealing work to be done for the child.

As research accelerated and increasing numbers of names were cleared for temple work, the highway between the Riverton Wyoming Stake and the Ogden Utah Temple became familiar territory to individuals, families, and groups of ward members seeking the spiritual rescue of their handcart friends. Even senior citizens entered the baptismal font for handcart pioneers they had come to know and love. Many stake members who had never been to the temple, or who hadn't attended for many years, were now making themselves worthy to enter the House of the Lord and participate in these holy ordinances. The stake presidency was thrilled to realize that between August 1991 and September 1992, eighty-two new temple recommends had been issued.

President Lorimer described the scope of the influence of the Second Rescue on members of his stake: "You would see people who were farmers and fishermen and cowboys—tough people, tough characters—stand at the pulpit and just weep about what had happened to them, [describing] the feelings they had felt and expressing thankfulness that they had been able to participate.

"[For example,] we have a man up in Dubois, Ron Rose, who is a fisherman. He goes up to Alaska and fishes in the summers. He accepted the challenge to do the [Second Rescue] work. He knew absolutely nothing about computers and didn't want to, but came down with his wife and started to look, and just became completely engulfed with the whole thing.

"On his first trip down to the Ogden Temple, he went with his brother-in-law and sister-in-law, Ron and Bonnie Titterington, and they had the intention of doing one endowment session. But they were in the temple that day for ten hours. He wouldn't leave. He came back home and just keeps repeating his journey back down [to the Ogden Temple]. I later processed 282 ordinances for family names for the two families through the TempleReady program. It just goes on and on." (Lorimer Oral Interview, p. 23.)

The Second Rescue project touched the lives of members of every age, every background, and in every corner of the stake. President Lorimer tells of the influence of the spirit of Elijah on the Lamanite members of the Wind River Branch: "Out on the reservation . . . the Wind River Branch has always been hesitant to be involved in Pioneer Day [celebrations] because they don't have any pioneers of Lamanite descent. But they really got involved in this project. I mean, they were dead serious about these Willie and Martin people. They learned how to do it. Now, they've discovered that there are 150 years of records on the reservation of their [own Lamanite] ancestors and they are processing Shoshone and Arapaho names for their own people. They have a very strong tie to their ancestry. As they feel the spirit of Elijah and do the work for their dead, I'm convinced that their reservation will never be the same." (Lorimer Oral Interview, p. 21.)

The spirit of Elijah was particularly noticeable to Ogden Temple officiators. President Dorman Baird noticed a strong spiritual feeling in the temple while the handcart names were being processed and attributed it to the devotion of members of the Riverton stake. "They brought such a special spirit with them to the temple because they had worked so hard to prepare to come do that work. It [was] so meaningful for them because they themselves had done the research for these pioneers. We just made the temple available to them [and] provided the services they needed. . . . We stayed late, if needed, to do sealings so they could do them while they

GEORGE CUNNINGHAM

One night at a campfire, fifteen-year-old George shared with other members of the Willie company a dream he had had the night before in which he had seen "that a number of wagons loaded with provisions were soon to meet us. How joyfully I related my last night's dream in detail. My mother told them that she knew it would come true, as I was promised that gift in my blessing. And to our great pleasure every word was literally fulfilled. I can recollect that I was in the lead of the crowd, feeling quite inspired by my dream. At their approach I roared out, 'See! See them coming over that hill!' We soon met the wagons with provisions and were very kindly treated and all felt to thank God."

George Cunningham, in "The Handcart Pioneers," in Kate B. Carter, comp., *Treasures of Pioneer History*, 6 vols. Salt Lake City: Daughters of Utah Pioneers, 1956, 5:252–56.

were here without having to make an additional trip. We tried to make it as convenient as possible [for them]." (Baird Taped Interview.)

Brother Robert Memmott, the temple recorder, echoed similar convictions: "There is a feeling that comes to the temple in relation to the preparation the people who come have made. Those participating in the Second Rescue came with a spirit that I would say was similar to the spirit of the Willie and Martin hand-cart people. You read their journals and you don't see much murmuring. You see a willingness to submit to the will of the Lord.

"[When] the Riverton people came here to the Ogden Temple, things were not always perfect. [But] they never complained. They were meek, they were mild, they were submissive. Their only desire was to serve the Lord. Their spirit just touched my heart. They never came and [insisted], 'Do this for us.' They came and in humility asked, 'Can you help us?'" (Memmott Taped Interview.)

The Riverton stake members in turn felt real close-

The Ogden Temple presidency with their wives. Left to right: Art and Colleen Checketts, Dorman and Lenora Baird, Dale and JoAnne Gardner.

ness to the Ogden Temple workers who showed such patience and love in accommodating their needs. President Lorimer spoke for many when he wrote: "The temple presidency, recorder, and temple workers of the Ogden Temple are to be highly complimented and praised for the great blessing they have been, for making this a tremendous spiritual experience for the members of our stake. They went out of their way to help make our members feel welcome, wanted, and appreciated at the temple. They were thorough and efficient in providing assistance in processing the names. . . . We have [all] truly worked 'hand in hand' with these faithful pioneers through a rich and abundant outpouring of the spirit of Elijah." ("History of the Second Rescue," written for the Ogden Temple history, 1992.)

Dee Lorimer, wife of President Scott Lorimer, echoed those feelings: "[The Ogden Temple officiators] treated us like royalty. President Baird and Brother Memmott will forever hold an honored place in our hearts for their kindness and help and understanding of what we were trying to do. It would have been impossible without them." (Letter to Susan Madsen, September 18, 1997.)

The Second Rescue was a resounding success. During the fourteen-month period from August 1991 to September 1992, more than 4,200 individual temple ordinances were completed in behalf of the Willie and Martin handcart pioneers, their 1856 rescuers, and their families. Overall, 52 percent of the temple ordinances for the Willie and Martin handcart pioneers and their rescuers needed to be completed.

In addition to baptisms and confirmations, children were sealed to their parents, husbands and wives were sealed for eternity, and the sacred covenants of the endowment were made in behalf of these handcart pioneers who gave so much for their testimonies of the restored gospel.

At the same time the research and temple work was being accomplished, the stake was also involved in building three monuments, making bronze plaques for those monuments and for the stake center, participating in handcart treks, and taking visiting General Authorities out to the rescue sites. It is impossible to calculate the enormous amount of time and commitment this project required. Many felt that the sheer organization of the project was nothing less than a miracle.

In spite of the crushing workload, stake members experienced a tremendous outpouring of the Spirit that would permanently affect their spiritual and temporal lives. During the year of the Second Rescue, the number of full-tithe payers increased 15 percent. Sacrament meeting attendance increased 6 percent. No disciplinary councils needed to be convened anywhere in the stake.

"And Should We Die," sculpture by Steve Wirth.

One of the most noticeable changes came in the number of Eagle Scout badges awarded within the stake. During the year before the Second Rescue, the entire Central Wyoming Council of the Boy Scouts of America awarded forty-one Eagle Scout badges. During the year of the Second Rescue, thirty-nine young men from the Riverton Wyoming Stake alone achieved Eagle Scout rank. Most of those young men have since filled honorable, full-time missions for the Church.

Even when the Second Rescue concluded, the spirit of Elijah lived on in the hearts of many of the stake members. The youth, for example, continued their search for ancestors—this time their own—in an enthusiastic and joyful way. After the Second Rescue project was completed, many youth continued to be baptized for names they had researched and submitted themselves. Years later, an average of 300 names per quarter were being added to the Riverton Wyoming Stake family file at the Ogden Temple.

Stake members found other ways to express their deep feelings about participating in the Second Rescue. Roadshows and pageants were written and produced. Booklets, original music, and poetry relating to the handcart pioneers were written. People continued to bear testimony of the ways their lives had been touched and changed by their newfound understanding of temple work.

Two talented artists, Steve Wirth and Philip Nebeker, each created a bronze sculpture depicting handcart pioneers. Those bronzes have deeply touched the hearts and souls of those who have seen them.

Steve Wirth's sculpture portrays the burial of ten-year-old Bodil Mortensen, the young Danish girl who died at Rock Creek Hollow, and the ascent of her spirit into the next life assisted by an angel. A photograph of the original sculpture appeared in the *Church News* on August 22, 1992. Bronze copies are found in homes and offices in Wyoming and Utah, as well as in the Church Office Building in Salt Lake City.

"Trail of Tears," sculpture by Philip Nebeker.

The story of the sculpture made by Philip Nebeker has its roots in a hunting incident that could have had a tragic ending. In October 1992, when Phil was seventeen years old, he was hunting elk with two friends in the Wind River Mountain Range. A sudden severe snowstorm blew in and the young men became disoriented and lost. They were found by Search and Rescue teams after being out in the cold for eighteen hours. Fortunately, they experienced only limited frostbite.

After such a terrifying, humbling experience, Phil felt new appreciation for the suffering of the Willie and Martin handcart companies. He felt inspired to create an art piece to honor them. Although Phil had relatively little sculpting experience, he had previously done some carving that had brought him recognition in a local art contest.

At about this same time, Phil wanted very much to serve a mission for the Church. However, with his older brother already serving full-time in Bulgaria, he knew his parents would have difficulty financing another missionary in the family. He felt sure that if he worked hard on his artwork, he could eventually earn enough money to pay for his mission without needing any outside financial assistance.

Phil created a sculpture depicting Bodil Mortensen and James Kirkwood, two young members of the Willie company. His experience of being lost in extreme cold weather was still vivid in his mind, and he was able to sculpt with true empathy. Proceeds from the sale of his work ultimately helped finance his mission to Portugal.

Clearly, the fruits of the Second Rescue were many and varied: the far-reaching effects of the temple work itself; the effect on the spirituality of the Saints of the Riverton Wyoming Stake; the effect on the Ogden Utah Temple workers; the increase in tithing faithfulness, sacrament meeting attendance, and the number of Eagle Scout awards earned; the participation of friends of other faiths; the creation of booklets, books, music, poetry, roadshows, pageants, and sculptures; and the strengthening of personal testimonies of young and old, active and less active.

Having seen all these things come to pass, the Saints who participated in the Second Rescue can testify from personal experience of the truthfulness and importance of the words Church President Howard W. Hunter spoke on November 13, 1994: "I have been deeply touched by the sacred spirit of [family history] work and by the thinness of the veil that separates the labor on this side from that which unfolds beyond. Who can calculate the great good that has been accomplished by so many faithful Saints who have worked in [this cause] through the years?

"I have one overriding message: This work must hasten. The work waiting to be done is staggering and escapes human comprehension. . . . [But] surely the Lord will support us if we use our best efforts in carrying out the commandment to do family history research and temple work. The great work of the temples and all that supports it must expand. It is imperative!" (*Ensign*, March 1995, pp. 64–65.)

The faithful Wyoming Saints felt the urgency of this work and participated valiantly in it, each giving what he or she could. They blessed the lives of the handcart pioneers, reaped blessings for themselves and their families, and laid a spiritual foundation that will bless generations to come.

CHAPTER 9

TESTIMONIALS

"I had never felt anything like that before."
NICHOLAS ZENT, AGE 12

IN THE FALL OF 1992, THE RIVERTON WYOMING Stake presidency asked each individual who participated in the Second Rescue to write down his or her memories and testimonies of the experience. Hundreds of stake members responded, and their writings were collected, bound, and placed in the Riverton stake center. This chapter includes a small sample of those testimonials. Some have been edited for clarity and readability. Ages are given for the children and teenagers whose testimonies are included.

Bertha Albright—Riverton Second Ward

Every Tuesday and Thursday morning, I went to the family history library from 7 A.M. until noon. I had time to read many of the handcart diaries that kept piling up in the library. I felt the tragic hopelessness of their plight, the freezing cold of Wyoming snow, the gnawing hunger, the heartache of fathers with families, the tears of mothers with little children.

I shall have a picture in my mind forever of me standing on my porch in the snow, the temperature below zero, frost hanging in the air, ice crunching under my feet, looking down at my warm gloves, my warm boots, feeling the warmth of my fleece-lined jacket and wishing somehow that I could share all of this with them. I appreciated, in a way I never had before, the comfort of my home, the plenty and variety of the food I had to eat, the luxuries I enjoyed. Never again will I envy those who have more than I of material things. I will always remember those Saints who had so little.

My daughter, Roberta, and I walked up on the hill where the Willie Rescue Site monument stands, read the inscription, and looked across the valley below where those Saints had camped, had huddled in their tents, had gazed upon the snowbound scene, had shivered and grieved and prayed. An overwhelming sense of sadness fell over me—sorrow and love. I could not speak. I felt them there even more than I had through the winter months searching out their stories. "How did you feel up there?" I asked Roberta. "Teary," she said. "I feel they are here."

The blessing came to me, of course, when I went to the temple and knelt at the altar as proxy for some of those who had suffered on the plains—and shared the joy with others who had searched the records and found enough information to do the temple work. There were tears there, too, and hearts so full we could not speak, but the spirit there was one of joy.

Justin Parks, age 6

Gerald and Debra Anderson—Riverton Second Ward

It was very satisfying watching our children, Beth and Scott, grow and mature in the gospel as the Second Rescue was taking place. At the time the research was being conducted, Beth was ten years old and Scott was eight years old. Their young age did not stop them from wanting to help with the research and wanting to be in the family history library when the information was found. They took turns on the computer and helped search the *Thornton* ship log. Scott's comment when he first saw the log was, "Why did they write something so important with such bad handwriting?"

Since Beth was not old enough to go into the temple, she came up with a fantastic solution. She wanted to have a family trip planned to go to the temple after she turns twelve to do baptismal work for her Dad's ancestors. Many prayers of gratitude were offered by her Mom and Dad for the Spirit of Elijah she was feeling. The night she presented the temple trip idea, we overheard her nightly prayer. It brought tears of joy to us [to hear her ask] her Father in Heaven to help her stay worthy to go to the temple.

Bishop Gary Anderson— Riverton Second Ward

After the special meeting was held that introduced the Second Rescue effort, our bishopric decided that all of the handcart names assigned to our ward would be placed in the members' care to research the following week. However, we decided that several of the names would be held back for families not in attendance that Sunday. I was concerned for the pioneers for whom research work would not begin immediately. However, through prayer I received confirmation that those pioneers felt it a privilege to be held in reserve for the strengthening of testimonies. I learned very quickly that the faith, testimonies, and unselfishness of the pioneers extends from the other side of the veil. . . .

Melinda Nelson, age 8

At the conclusion of the dedication of the Willie Rescue Site, August 15, 1992, just as the closing song "Come, Come, Ye Saints" was beginning, President Lorimer patted President Kitchen on the knee and they stood up together. While standing, President Lorimer put his arm around President McKinnon as he stood. He also had his other arm around President Kitchen. For a brief moment, the stake presidency stood side by side with President Lorimer having his arms around the other brethren's shoulders. What an impact that sequence of events had on me. There were no personal agendas involved in this rescue. Only the will of Heavenly Father influenced the events of the Second Rescue. The unity of these brethren has spread throughout the stake, thus making the Riverton Wyoming Stake a stronger stake.

Bishop Melvin Baldwin—Riverton Second Ward

The Second Rescue of the Willie and Martin handcart companies was a tremendous opportunity for our family to participate in an activity of eternal consequence. We gladly accepted the challenge of an inspired stake president and worked with diligence to research our assigned families, the David Reeder family and Ann Jane Thomas.

We cried together as we read the journals that described David Reeder, lovingly called Grandfather Reeder, as he gave his pitifully small daily food rations to his grandchildren and then finally died of malnutrition and exposure on the trail near Ft. Laramie, Wyoming. What a wonderful example to myself as the patriarch of my own family to know of his total willingness to give everything that he had to see that his children and grandchildren could get to Zion.

Our oldest daughter, Nikki, was totally consumed with the need to research Ann Jane Thomas. After many tears, much hard work, and many prayers, Nikki was able to find the necessary documentation so that she could be baptized and confirmed for Ann Thomas. As her mother and I observed the tears of joy as Nikki acted as proxy, we knew that the veil was very thin that morning and that Nikki and Ann were truly sisters in the gospel.

Tia Barrus (age 12)—Riverton Second Ward

My older brother and sister had the chance to go on the youth handcart trek. After they were done and back home, they went straight to bed. They had bad sunburns, blisters on their feet, and a stronger testimony of the Church. Truthfully, I thought it was worth it.

Maureen Day—Riverton Second Ward

During the past year our lives have been touched in a special way. We have been married almost thirty years and our own temple work had not been done. During the Second Rescue we were asked to attend temple preparation classes. We were pleased to have this opportunity. On June 27, 1992, after many prayers were answered, we received our own endowments and were married for eternity along with having Julie Ann sealed to us in the Idaho Falls Temple. I was also sealed to my parents. How very blessed and thankful we are to have had the opportunity to take a small part in this inspired project of the Second Rescue.

Matthew Bills, age 7

Bishop Frank Enos—Lander First Ward

At the temple, I performed all ordinances for Johann Ahmanson. I felt nothing until the temple worker bestowed the Melchizedek Priesthood on me in behalf of Johann. A strong spiritual impression came over me and I began to weep. I felt he was there and was thankful that I had done this for him. I believe my life will never be the same.

Cory Fabrizius (age 15)—Riverton Second Ward

President Lorimer and my Dad, Ron, were talking after church every Sunday. The short chats turned into short meetings and then the short meetings turned into long meetings. I learned that President Lorimer and my Dad were going to attempt to make some bronze plaques. They had many problems getting everything ready. I remember how my Dad struggled every night after work making tools and designing a kiln. It took a long time for him to get everything ready. Finally everything was finished and ready to go. We had many failures in those weeks. Too many to list. It was the week of the dedication. We all said a prayer in the shop that all would work. You could say that my faith was a bit shaken every time we cast a bronze that did not work. Finally we had a plaque that turned out. The plaques we made turned out beautiful. It came down to the last two days. I helped install the plaque at Rocky Ridge along with my Grandpa, Bishop Anderson, Pete Peterson, and Chuck Carper and his wife, Cindy.

I want to thank my parents for letting me be a part of the Second Rescue. I love them and I also love my whole family and how they all participated in the rescue.

Lisa Fabrizius (age 11)—Riverton Second Ward

I felt special because I got to help with the monuments. I helped by babysitting my two younger brothers, Ryan and Eric, and by cleaning the house each day while my parents were working on the bronze plaques. . . .

When the kids were coming in from the handcart trek I felt like I could see the pioneers coming with the snow on their coats.

Rick Fagnant—Lander First Ward

An unexpected lump consumed my throat as the ceremonies at the Willie Rescue Site began. Seeing 1,400 Latter-day Saints sitting on blankets in the middle of the desert, seeing the youth reenact the handcart companies, seeing the monument that required many hours of skilled laborers' time to erect, and listening to President Hinckley, for some reason, made me realize for the first time the significance the early pioneers played in the building of the Church. I am a convert to the Church. My testimony is special to me. The saints who died so that we could exercise our beliefs are special. I can not wait to meet them and thank them.

Brittany Smith, age 5

Barbara Fournier—Riverton First Ward

Because of the Second Rescue all is well for those who made the trip across the west. Thanks for the blessings.

Rhonda Fowler—Lander Second Ward

I wondered sometimes if I'd looked at the computer too long when I shopped at IGA and made my check out to the IGI [International Genealogical Index].

Donna Gard—Riverton First Ward

For years, since I was a child of six, I have held the grave site of the Willie handcart pioneers at Rock Creek sacred in my heart. What a thrill it was to send off a young pioneer on a memorial trek this year. Tears came to my eyes the next day as we heard the shout, "Here they come!"

Kristen Gard (age 12)—Riverton First Ward

The youth got to go to the temple and got baptized for the dead. The spirits of the pioneers were really strong and encouraging. Once we got out of the temple their spirits seemed to evaporate. I wanted to go back into the temple.

Bishop Mike Gard—Riverton First Ward

The Willie and Martin pioneers rejoiced in the truth, bore all things this earthly life could give, believed all things, hoped for all things, and endured all things. In death and more importantly in life they demonstrated a pure love of Christ. I do not know them by sight, but they know me, and I count them as my friends.

After pulling the handcarts 20 miles this summer, we were received by approximately 1,000 members of our stake. To my surprise they stood as one and cheered and clapped as the first carts arrived and continued until all were in. Shouts of joy rent the air. Families were joined together again and joyful tears were all around. [It was] a feeling I shall never forget. My prayer has been that I will pull on the cart of this life hard enough that I might repeat this scene on the other side of the veil.

Sarah Gard (age 15)—Riverton First Ward

My favorite part was going on the trek. I thought it would be pretty easy, but as the day progressed I started to change my mind. I started to think about the pioneers and how they did the same thing day after day. When it was time for lunch and I was given a roll and cheese, I thought I would never get full. When we made camp I was ready for bed, but as soon as the program started I was having too much fun to sleep.

Benjamin S. Gibson (age 15)—Riverton Second Ward

As president of the teachers quorum, I had the duty of looking over the members of my quorum on the youth handcart trek. There were about 15 teachers from my quorum on the trek. If they were injured or disabled in any way, it was my responsibility to help them overcome and finish. No one in the quorum was hurt. Richie McKinnon, however, got sick the second morning but was well by the time we left. I said a prayer before we left and asked that all the sick would be healed and that no one would get hurt. No one got hurt and Richie was better within 30 minutes.

Kara Harrison (age 10)—Riverton Second Ward

My Dad, who served with the stake presidency as stake clerk, would come home late every Sunday night from working on the Willie and Martin handcart project. He would go to the church at 7:00 in the morning and often not get home until 10:00 at night. He would go straight to the kitchen to get some food when he would come home. One Sunday the whole high council was going to spend the entire day working on the project. I got permission from President Lorimer to organize my Merrie Miss Class into bringing food in to them so they would have more energy to keep working. This was for my Gospel in Action Award. I really felt good about helping others out because they spent so much time working on the project for the benefit of all of us.

Kathy Huff—Lander Second Ward

The Second Rescue . . . was a very special experience for me. Seeing my sixteen-year-old son be baptized for his great-grandfather and later hearing him relate the experience to his older sister as the "best part of the trip" to Ogden is a feeling that a mother can not express in words.

Buddy Ivie (age 15)—Shoshoni Branch

The most spiritual thing I experienced was the trip of about 300 miles we took to be baptized for the pioneers. There was a very humble feeling that I felt when the man that baptized me read the name of the pioneer that was waiting to get his work done. I will never forget that feeling.

Ashley Smith, age 7

President John L. Kitchen, Jr.—Lander First Ward

I am grateful to my Father in Heaven for this opportunity to do a small part in this great work, and to witness the changes that have taken place in so many lives. What a blessing this has been. I am grateful for the devotion of the high council, the bishops and branch presidents as they have been asked to go the second mile. There was no hesitation, they just did it. There are many in the stake who went way beyond what they were called to do both in research and in the erection of the monuments. I am grateful to be associated with them.

Adam Lowell Larsen (age 11)—Lander First Ward

Even though I only poured cement, unloaded rock, and set up the podium, it still was fun.

Ben Smith, age 9

John Larsen—Lander First Ward

It did not matter whether it was digging and pouring the foundation, pouring the cap, or getting the native rock at La Barge Creek, there was always a good spirit with those that were working on the [monuments] project. We had a lot of fun and gained a great respect for the early pioneers.

Bishop Lloyd Larsen—Lander First Ward

Going out to work on the monuments I would tell my four sons why we were doing the work, and every time I would cry. As I would drive in that area and think about [the pioneers] there would always be a reverent feeling come over me, leaving me with a humble feeling that I would always like to have. During these feelings my mind painted very clear pictures of these good saints and it was not so much what I could see, but more the way I felt that has left me to believe that perhaps I do know them.

Desiree Lorimer—Riverton Second Ward

As the wife of President Robert Scott Lorimer, I rejoiced with him when the answer finally came that the Second Rescue was not about the land, but rather it was about the temple work. Goosebumps covered me as I realized that he had indeed received a revelation and knew that what was happening was bigger than we had ever imagined. Did I ever doubt it? No! For I know the man! Never have I known anyone who could be more trusted by the Lord or by anyone. He lives his life every day in such a way that I KNEW what he said was true.

How can I express the feelings I had as I listened to him pray at night by our bedside for the members of the stake? We have rejoiced at the increased activity of the stake members. As a wife this meant I said good-bye even more often as he performed more and more temple recommend interviews and wrote more letters and visited more people.

I will never forget the night [our daughter] Autumn answered the phone and it turned out to be President Gordon B. Hinckley, of the First Presidency. I wonder if he will ever know the wonder and awe he inspired in us? How we were so humbled that this great servant of God would understand and care about what we were doing here in the middle of Wyoming! How he gave us the courage to keep going.

I have marveled at the beautiful talents of the people of this stake. Scott has been very inspired in choosing people and letting them use their special skills throughout the entire year. It was not "President Lorimer's project." It belonged to all the members of the stake. Consequently all of the members of the stake grew spiritually, and never has the stake been so unified. . . .

The Second Rescue is spiritual and powerful but it is also personal. We believe in revelation. We believe in life after death. We believe that we are led by a real prophet. We believe in sacrifice and hard work and following and supporting our leaders in a humble but prayerful way. The Second Rescue is all of those things. It changes people. I have seen it in the lines that go on for hours every time we speak. I have felt it in the hundreds of phone calls I have answered as people cry and laugh and pour out their hearts to me because they are related to a handcart pioneer or they were simply touched by the spirit of what they had read about or heard about. I have experienced modern-day miracles. I know it and so does everyone else who was involved.

This chapter of our lives is over, but the effects will never end unless we forget. . . . Now surely, we must not rest or ever be the same as we were before.

Heika Lorimer (age 11)—Riverton Second Ward

I went to church with just my scriptures but walked out with a huge smile and a packet with James Alfred Peacock's name written on it. My Dad and I could not find him on the computer so we ordered some microfilm. We searched for a very long time and we did not find him. Just when we were about to stop we both felt that we should keep going. We were both so excited when we finally found him that we both let out a big happy yell.

When President and Sister Hinckley came to eat dinner with us there was such a wonderful feeling in the house that I barely wanted to breathe in fear I would ruin it. His security man was really funny and President Hinckley and his wife were just like grandparents.

Kelly Lorimer (age 3)—Riverton Second Ward

Kelly was asked in an interview, "What is the Second Rescue?" Her response was, "It is where my Dad works. He does lots of important stuff there for the pioneers."

Luke Lorimer (age 9)—Riverton Second Ward

I am grateful that I had the opportunity of working on the waxes for the monuments. I am grateful that my little sister and I were not hurt when we heated the wax so my family could pour it into the rubber molds every day. I really enjoyed President Hinckley coming to dinner and showing us how to take care of our trees.

Kevin McNiven—Wind River Branch

I have learned why in the second section of the Doctrine and Covenants the Lord said, "I will reveal unto you the Priesthood, by the hand of Elijah the Prophet." It is one thing to receive the priesthood but quite another to have it revealed to you.

While in the temple I was wondering who received more blessings—the people we had done the life-saving ordinances for, or if I had received the greater blessing because of the life-saving light and knowledge granted to me because of the endowments we had participated in.

President Kim McKinnon—Riverton Second Ward

As I have been blessed to process many of the names through

TempleReady, I have felt the Spirit guiding my thoughts and actions. I have been led to research and have had unfold before me family relationships that would not have been apparent to a conventional researcher. I have been led to names which needed to be taken to the temple; I have had the Spirit direct my research to names I would not have otherwise considered. It is my testimony that this project has occurred under the direction of the Spirit. He has guided and inspired hundreds within our stake and many outside of the stake. We have been successful to the degree we have complied with the inspiration given. We have been collectively and individually moved upon by forces which have guided our thoughts and controlled our actions. The credit for the success of this venture, the appreciation for being part of it goes to the Lord, who has allowed us by His grace to be the instrumentality of its fulfillment.

Holly Yardas, age 6

William Miller—Riverton First Ward

My family was given the Peter Moss family to research. We did the research and found that much of the work had been done. There were a total of thirty ordinances that still needed to be done. While I was in the temple doing baptisms it became clear to me at that at least one of the persons for whom I was doing the work was very excited about it. I may never know this person in this life. All I know is that someone was there with me and watching the baptisms. I do not pretend to receive inspiration for the stake but the witness I received was that my family and I in our various callings and in our family's work in doing the research was the work of our Heavenly Father and that He was pleased.

Barbara Moon—Riverton First Ward

With a lump in my throat, I watched the youth again pull the handcarts up a long hill to welcome President and Sister Hinckley. It was as though the handcart people were there with us, pulling the carts again, only this time with great joy.

Cami Packer (age 17)—Lander First Ward

My pioneer's name was Mary. I made sure the work for her was completed. Mary was from England, and although she survived the trek across the plains, she died at a young age. She was a few years older than me when she came across the plains. On our handcart trek I thought about her frequently. I still hold in my memory a girl named Mary, perhaps a lot like me, who sacrificed everything for the gospel and her testimony of it. I can hardly wait to meet and talk with her. If I were asked to endure the same trials as Mary [did], my answer would be a resounding "YES."

Kati Packer (age 8)—Lander First Ward

I felt sorry and sad for the pioneers and what they went through. I wondered how they went over Rocky Ridge with the babies. When I went over and looked at the monument I felt really good that I am a child of God.

Carolyn Pence (age 17)—Riverton Second Ward

Last year when President Lorimer first approached our stake and told us of his feelings for these people and how he had come to know of their need for our help, I was touched and awed at his great spirituality and our responsibility to these people who were actually depending on us to do

Meri Galloway, age 8

what they could not do for themselves. That meeting was, without a doubt, one of the most spiritual experiences of my life, and I, along with all else in attendance, can testify that the spirit felt that day was wonderfully strong and heartening. That spirit, of those people for whom we were to serve, gave us the determination and the desire to do what had been asked of us.

I look forward to the day when I will return to the Father across the veil and actually meet these special people who have helped me gain a better and stronger testimony of the true and everlasting gospel of Jesus Christ.

Jacqueline Scott—Lander First Ward

I am a genealogy librarian, and we quickly learned the use of the computer and discovered the things we needed to know in order to help others do their assigned names. It was magnificent to be there as the brothers and sisters worked at the library. We witnessed their happiness and surprise, widened eyes and smiles as they found the information they needed. Then we heard their sincere testimonies later.

Jacob Paul Smith (age 16)—Lander Second Ward

After the dedication I got to shake President Hinckley's hand. As I shook his hand it felt different than shaking anybody else's hand. I went to the fireside that night—he was shaking people's hands on the side rows and I moved my sister closer to him so she could feel the feeling too. He shook Abby's hand.

Tyson Dana Miller Taylor (age 8)—Lander Second Ward

At the dedication I helped pass out water to people in the crowd. It was a hot day and it was fun to help. I listened to President Hinckley. After the program I got to shake his hand. I thought it was neat. I told him my name. He is a good man.

Bonnie Titterington—Dubois Branch

I remember the inadequate feelings the first time we went to use the computer in Riverton. We came away with no new information the first several 160-mile round trips we made. We fought down feelings of discouragement and despair. Then on one of the many trips my daughter-in-law Janean punched a button on the computer and there was my Margery Smith with a husband and all the children except the oldest child Margery! I had been right—the oldest son was named after his father. It was wonderful and we drove home late that night—happy, happy people. . . .

The most excited I became is when President Lorimer placed our disk in the computer and it started accepting all kinds of work that needed to be done! I wanted to jump up and down and slap President Lorimer on the back and shout for joy. It was all I could do to remain seated and act like a lady.

Morris Trover—Riverton Second Ward

Several times during my stay here in Wyoming I have had an opportunity to walk or ride along the great pioneer trail and several times I have stopped and closed my eyes and could hear trace chains, iron wagon wheels on rocks, cattle and horse noises, and muffled voices of men, women, and children as they progressed along the trail. I have always respected the will and faith and strength of the pioneer people and tried to test myself to see if I had what it would have taken to be there with them.

Bev Whiting—Lander Second Ward

When we got to the temple baptistry, I saw two sisters (sisters by birth) from our ward, neither of whom has been endowed, waiting to do baptisms for their Second Rescue names. I asked permission to give my one female name to one of them. Afterwards I was able to visit with them briefly. They had traveled 300 miles that morning to each do the baptism for the one name they had researched and were making the 300-mile return trip to Lander immediately after leaving the temple. They traveled over 600 miles to do one baptism each.

Vicky Yardas—Lander First Ward

After the Second Rescue meeting one of my dear friends came up to me and asked, "How are you going to complete the work for your names?" I did not know, but I did know that I could at least do the baptism and confirmation. I shall never forget when Sister Alice Gee handed me our family names. A warm, special feeling went completely through me. We were slow in doing the research because we had never done genealogy before.

Brandon Howell

On May 22, 1992, I received one of the greatest blessings of my life. I will be eternally grateful to my nonmember husband for giving me permission to go to the temple to receive my own endowments. I feel and know that this blessing was a direct result of my involvement in the Second Rescue of the Willie and Martin people. It provided a way for me to accept the endowment for Castina Brown.

On June 20, 1992, I had the opportunity to go with the youth to the temple. Lori, my daughter, was baptized for Castina and Jane Brown. I was confirmed for Castina, Jane, and Anne Anderson. When I went to do the initiatory work and they were closed for the day, I was disappointed and told them I would come back. The dear sister that was there said, "No, you have the right to do that work." She found two sisters to assist me. During and after the ordinance the tears of appreciation would not stop. As I dressed I could not quit sobbing. I was so grateful to be a part of the work.

Nicholas Zent (age 12)—Shoshoni Branch

The thing that I remember the most about the Second Rescue of the

Bridget Wilkinson, age 11

Willie and Martin Handcart Companies was the trip I took with the stake presidency. I rode with Bishop Maddock to Independence Rock. We saw the names of the pioneers that crossed the plains. We then drove to Devil's Gate and a place called Martin's Cove. The spirit that was felt as we walked around can not be described in words. It was very calm on one side but when I walked over the hill I got this feeling I can not explain. When I stood on a certain rock I could almost see the pioneers walking in the cold and snow. I had never felt anything like that before.

CHAPTER 10

ROCK CREEK HOLLOW

"Rock Creek would not leave me alone."

PRESIDENT R. SCOTT LORIMER

ROCK CREEK HOLLOW WAS THE BIRTHPLACE OF the Second Rescue of the Willie and Martin handcart companies. It was in this secluded pioneer campground that President Scott Lorimer first felt the stirrings of the Spirit whispering to him that a sacred project awaited members of the Riverton Wyoming Stake.

Just as Martin's Cove has come to symbolize the suffering and sacrifice of the Martin handcart company and the Hunt and Hodgett wagon trains, Rock Creek Hollow is a sacred symbol of the mighty price paid by members of the James G. Willie company in their struggle to gather with the Latter-day Saints in the Salt Lake Valley.

Located in central Wyoming, eight miles south of Atlantic City, Rock Creek Hollow was a two-day resting place for the approximately 460 surviving members of the Willie handcart company. When they pulled into the hollow on October 23, 1856, they had just completed a forced march up and across treacherous Rocky Ridge and down the western slope of South Pass.

President Lorimer spoke of these remarkable people on July 23, 1994, at the Rock Creek Hollow dedicatory service: "Truly the people who were here on October 23, 1856, were a cut above the norm. Captain Willie had not slept for three days, had not eaten much, but at midnight he was willing to leave the main company and go back and get others who were still far behind, struggling along. The forced march from the Willie rescue site to Rock Creek is only twelve miles. For us today it seems as though it is nothing. For members of the Willie company to go from the rescue site to Rock Creek took some of them twenty-seven hours in a blizzard, with shoes that were worn out, and on feet that were bleeding." (Meetings of the Second Rescue.)

Of those who survived the terrible ordeal and huddled at Rock Creek Hollow, many with frozen, blackened feet and hands, fifteen would be dead by the next morning. It is little wonder, then, that the Spirit of the Lord fills this place and rests mightily on those who visit with receptive and humble hearts.

Rock Creek Hollow

A man from Atlantic City, Wyoming, known only as "Old Man Carpenter," played an important role in the identification and preservation of the site by informing others of the historical importance of Rock Creek Hollow. During the early to mid-1900s, Mr. Carpenter tended the area, keeping alive the memory of the religious martyrs. Elder George Albert Smith, who would later become President of the Church, visited Wyoming in 1933 while serving as president of the Utah Pioneer Trails and Landmarks Association. He met Mr. Carpenter, who informed him of the significance of Rock Creek Hollow and the existence of the common grave.

Elder Smith then went to Rock Creek Hollow with representatives of the Lyman Wyoming Stake to find the grave. After two frustrating days of not being able to find the actual grave site, he invited his companions to kneel in prayer. A Bishop Rollins of Evanston was walking to where the prayer was to be held when he tripped and fell to the ground, hurting himself. Others from the party came to his assistance and found that he had tripped over the iron rim of a handcart wheel that was partially buried and hidden in the sagebrush.

Elder Smith knelt with the other brethren at the location where the mishap had occurred and received a spiritual confirmation that the wheel rim marked the location of the sacred grave. He arranged for a large boulder to be placed there to mark the spot. Later that year the Utah Pioneer Trails and Landmarks Association had a bronze marker mounted to the boulder. In subsequent years the Lyman and Rock Springs Wyoming stakes constructed a stone monument over the boulder and mounted the bronze plaque on it. With the exception of minor repairs due to cracking caused by winter freezing, the monument and plaque have remained undisturbed since that time.

Years passed, however, before many members of the Church knew the location or fully understood the spiritual and symbolic importance of the remote pioneer campsite and burial ground.

In time, descendants of those who suffered at Rock Creek Hollow in late October of 1856 became increasingly interested in the site. In 1979, for example, Paul Willie, a descendant of Captain James G. Willie, arranged for a granite marker to be made, engraved with the names and ages of those who are buried in the common grave as well as the two men buried nearby. Paul presented the marker to members of the Riverton stake during one of their annual July 24th campouts at Rock Creek Hollow. It was later installed at the grave as an Eagle Scout project.

President Lorimer knew from his first visit to the hollow with his young family in 1977 that there was something powerful and cleansing about the spirit he felt there. His continued and persistent response to that spirit set in motion events that would bring to light many significant aspects of the history of the Willie and Martin companies. Among other things, as a counselor in the stake presidency, President Lorimer received approval to hold Pioneer Day celebrations at the hollow. He also organized stake handcart treks from Rocky Ridge to Rock Creek Hollow and later, as stake president, encouraged and conducted research that would call attention to the historical importance of this long-neglected area.

Because of the success of the celebrations and the handcart treks, and

JOHN CHISLETT

"The day we crossed Rocky Ridge it was snowing a little—the wind hard from the north-west—and blowing so keenly that it almost pierced us through. We had to wrap ourselves closely in blankets, quilts, or whatever else we could get, to keep from freezing. . . . My duty was to stay behind everything and see that nobody was left along the road. . . . The ascent of the ridge commenced soon after leaving camp, and I had not gone far up it before I overtook a cart that the folks could not pull through the snow, here about knee-deep. I helped them along, and we soon overtook another. By all hands getting to one cart we could travel; so we moved one of the carts a few rods, and then went back and brought up the other. After moving in this way for a while, we overtook other carts at different points of the hill, until we had six carts, not one of which could be moved by the parties owning it. I put our collective strength to three carts at a time, took them a short distance, and then brought up the other three."

John Chislett narrative published in T.B.H. Stenhouse, *The Rocky Mountain Saints* (New York: D. Appleton, 1873).

ARCHIBALD MCPHAIL

Archibald McPhail was the leader of his tent and was put in charge of several single women. After they made the difficult journey over Rocky Ridge and into Rock Creek, Archibald noticed that one of his single sisters was missing, and he went back to look for her. He found her sitting on the other side of Strawberry Creek.

"He pleaded with her to come on, but she refused, saying she was going to stay there and die. There was nothing to do but cross the stream and get her. He picked her up and as they crossed the stream the ice broke and he was soaked with icy water to the waist.

"By the time he reached camp his clothes were frozen to him and he was taking heavy chills. The air was cold and wet and the men were so weak and hungry they could not go in search of dry wood to make a fire. Without anything warm to eat or drink, he was placed in a cold bed with the covering of a handcart pitched over him for a tent. There was a strong wind blowing which blew it over three times, and they stopped trying to keep it up. He was in high fever, and [his daughter] Henrietta sat by his bed brushing the snow from his face as he lay dying."

"Life Sketch of Henrietta McPhail Eckersell," by Mary Darley Harper. Typescript, Riverton Wyoming Stake Handcart Library.

the spiritual impact on those who participated, the Riverton stake presidency sought permission from Church leaders in Salt Lake City to pursue efforts to purchase Rock Creek Hollow from a private landowner. Their hope was that the land would become an official Church history site with permanent public access, and that the opportunity to visit Rock Creek Hollow and experience the spirit of its sacred history would be made available to all who were interested.

After prolonged negotiations, in which President Lorimer played a key role, contracts were executed and the Church's purchase of Rock Creek Hollow was finalized on September 9, 1992. Significantly, this agreement was reached just four days after the temple work was completed for the Willie and Martin handcart pioneers and their rescuers.

The summers of 1993 and 1994 were filled with the sounds of volunteers from the Riverton Wyoming Stake working to beautify Rock Creek Hollow. They leveled tailings from earlier mining activity, installed sprinkler pipes, and raked in grass seed and native flowers. Rock Creek Hollow blossomed, not only in green grasses and prairie flowers, but in the hearts of all who visited.

Several Eagle Scout projects beautified the area and made it more functional. These projects included three road signs in Atlantic City directing the way to Rock Creek, a fence around the common grave, two cattle guards, installation of a guest registry, and the construction of gates at the edges of the Church-owned property.

During the summer of 1994, a tragic motorcycle accident took the life of George Broce, a priest in the Riverton Second Ward. At the time of his death, George was only two merit badges short of the rank of Eagle. His priesthood quorum wanted to complete his Eagle requirements for him even though they were told he could not receive the award posthumously. They completed the merit badges and built a flagpole for his Eagle project. There is no plaque in memory of George, but a spirit of reverence surrounds the flagpole, which stands as a touching symbol of the commitment of the priests quorum to their fallen member.

Subsequent years brought several thousand visitors to Rock Creek Hollow. A 700-seat amphitheater to handle large groups was constructed as a father/son project. Even though the amphitheater itself was large enough, there was still not enough land to accommodate those who wished to spend time at Rock Creek. Additional acres were purchased to provide for parking, camping, permanent rest rooms, and a well. In President Lorimer's eyes, this was about as far as improvements could go without obscuring or destroying the fundamental nature of the site.

Amphitheater at Rock Creek Hollow

On July 23, 1994, President Gordon B. Hinckley, who at the time was First Counselor in the First Presidency of The Church of Jesus Christ of Latter-day Saints, was scheduled to officially dedicate Rock Creek Hollow and the mass grave located there. As part of the dedicatory services, the youth of the Riverton stake were asked to perform a special musical number. President Lorimer, acting on his long-standing feelings, requested that they sing "Learn of Me," a piece by Janice Kapp Perry and Joy Saunders Lundberg that is traditionally sung in the Young Women program.

Some people questioned the choice, wondering whether the young men would be willing to participate, but President Lorimer saw this as a potential teaching moment rather than an obstacle. When some resistance was felt, he reminded the young men that many young women of the stake had helped with Eagle projects knowing that they themselves could never

JOHN CHISLETT

John Chislett, a member of the Willie handcart company, described how the stranded Willie company received news that help was on the way:

"We traveled on in misery and sorrow day after day. Sometimes we made a pretty good distance, but at other times we were only able to make a few miles' progress. Finally we were overtaken by a snowstorm which the shrill wind blew furiously about us. The snow fell several inches deep as we traveled along, but we dared not stop, for we had a sixteen-mile journey to make, and short of it we could not get wood and water.

"As we were resting for a short time at noon a light wagon was driven into our camp from the west. Its occupants were Joseph A. Young and Stephen Taylor. They informed us that a train of supplies was on the way, and we might expect to meet it in a day or two. More welcome messengers never came from the courts of glory than these two young men were to us. They lost no time after encouraging us all they could to press forward, but sped on further east to convey their glad news to Edward Martin and the fifth handcart company who left Florence about two weeks after us, and who it was feared were even worse off than we were. As they went from our view, many a hearty 'God bless you!' followed them."

John Chislett narrative published in T.B.H. Stenhouse, *The Rocky Mountain Saints* (New York: D. Appleton, 1873).

aspire to the rank of Eagle Scout. Now the young men had a chance to participate in one of the Young Women traditions.

"I told them that I, as an Eagle Scout myself with three palms, would gladly trade the Scout Oath and Scout Laws for this sacred group of words and the piano accompaniment of 'Learn of Me,'" he later wrote. "I told the young men to go home, humble themselves, and find every young man in our stake who was not at the practice and get them there for the rest of the practices. I told the young women to also go and bring all the inactive and nonparticipating young women to the rest of the practices. . . .

"The next Sunday I was in a bishop's training meeting at about 8:00 P.M. when there was a very timid knock at the high council room door. My clerk answered it and brought me a message that one of our Young Women was there in tears and she wanted to know if I would like to come out on the lawn and see the choir practice. I excused myself from the meeting and began to go out. One of our high councilors caught me at the door and said they were practicing on the lawn as the dedication would be out-of-doors. I went to the front lawn of the chapel and saw a sight I will long remember. I saw more than 150 young men and young women all with red eyes from tears of joy and understanding because of this wonderful song. Although it was not required, every young man was dressed in a white shirt and tie and was grateful to the Young Women for the opportunity of being there. Of the youth there Sunday night there were several nonmember young men and young women." (Letter from R. Scott Lorimer to Janette C. Hales, July 12, 1994.)

Such teaching moments seemed to grow regularly out of events associated with the Second Rescue.

The efforts of the Saints of the Riverton Wyoming Stake in beautifying Rock Creek Hollow are already bearing impressive fruits in the lives of others. During the year of 1997 alone, 42,000 people signed the register at Rock Creek Hollow and about 27,000 camped there overnight.

A new and imposing monument at Rock Creek Hollow was dedicated on July 26, 1997, as the culminating event at the Riverton stake Pioneer Day celebration held that year. It memorializes the Second Rescue and the blessings associated with it. The inscription on the six-foot-high, eight-ton granite stone reads:

> To the People of
> The Second Rescue
> REMEMBER
> Gordon B. Hinckley
> August 15, 1992
> Thomas S. Monson
> July 15, 1997
> James E. Faust
> July 25, 1992
> Helaman 10:4–5

The names are those of the First Presidency of The Church of Jesus Christ of Latter-day Saints. On August 15, 1992, President Hinckley dedicated the monuments at Martin's Cove, the Willie rescue site, and Rocky Ridge and pronounced a sacred blessing on the people of the stake. On July 15, 1997, President Thomas S. Monson spoke to over 1,400 people in a meeting held in Riverton and gave them a special blessing. And on July 25, 1992, the youth and later the entire membership of the Riverton Wyoming Stake received powerful blessings from Elder James E. Faust. The monument at Rock Creek Hollow stands as a mighty reminder and urges the people of the Second Rescue to REMEMBER the words, promises, and blessings of the Lord through his apostles and prophets to them.

President Gordon B. Hinckley stands beside monument at Rock Creek Hollow.

THE MONUMENTS AND BRONZE PLAQUES

*"Nothing but the best was good enough for the
Martin and Willie handcart people."*
PRESIDENT R. SCOTT LORIMER

FEW TIMES DURING THE SECOND RESCUE project was the faith and endurance of the Riverton Wyoming Stake Latter-day Saints tested more keenly than during the building of three monuments honoring the pioneers. This aspect of the project began in October 1991 with President Scott Lorimer's feelings that there should be a monument of some kind at Martin's Cove to commemorate the people who suffered and died there for the gospel's sake. The monument should also pay tribute, he said, to the enormously important rescue effort organized by President Brigham Young. Support for the idea was enthusiastic and universal. In time, the plan was expanded to include two additional monuments, one in the vicinity of the Willie handcart company rescue site and the other at the summit of Rocky Ridge.

Interestingly enough, and beyond coincidence, Gary Long, an employee of the Federal Bureau of Land Management (BLM) in Lander, Wyoming, telephoned President Lorimer that very month regarding efforts to restore the Mormon Trail in the area of the handcart rescue sites. He wondered, would the Riverton people be interested in helping with the restoration? President Lorimer suggested the three monuments, and Gary Long invited him to submit plans for approval.

The effort to design and build three monuments and to cast bronze plaques for them was thus launched, and in its own way proved to be nothing short of heroic. President Lorimer felt strongly about having the monuments and plaques constructed and manufactured within the boundaries of the Riverton Wyoming Stake. He later explained why:

"I had discussed the possibility of building monuments with various individuals in the Church Historical Department. They suggested that we use anodized aluminum plaques. I really did not want to do so, as it seemed that we were not doing a good enough job for the Willie and Martin handcart pioneers. Nothing was too good for them. I wanted bronze plaques just like the old monuments had. I was told that the cost was prohibitive and that we could not afford them. My research verified what I had been told.

"We already had done so many things that I felt we could do anything. I therefore rationalized that if we donated the labor, we could significantly reduce the cost. I felt strongly that we would have wonderful experiences and would be blessed. I knew we could do it." (Letter to Susan Madsen, September 26, 1997.)

As was always the case when a new phase of the Second Rescue began, those with the skills and knowledge to accomplish the task came forward when needed and were eager and willing to work the projects through to completion.

Dan Barrus drew the designs for the monuments, which were to be similar in appearance to the existing monument at Rock Creek Hollow, constructed in 1933 by the Lyman Wyoming Stake. Each of the three new monuments would be built to endure, and would weigh from nine to twelve tons. As President Lorimer commented, "They won't be going any-where."

By May of 1992, committee members had selected—and the BLM had approved—the construction sites. Volunteers, some of whom had to travel more than two hours just to reach the sites, were working simultaneously on the foundations of all three monuments. President Lorimer remembers: "We'd announce Sunday morning, 'This Saturday we're going to do this and that on the monuments . . .' and there were so many people up there [Saturday morning] you were stumbling over yourself trying to get the work done. People just wanted to be involved." (Lorimer Oral History, p. 40.)

Volunteers of all ages, male and female, prepared the ground, built forms, and poured footings and a concrete base. The four walls of each monument were made of cement block laid so as to allow steel rebar embedded in the foundation to pass through the interior of the blocks. The cement blocks were then filled with concrete, thus attaching the walls to the footings. The cavity within the walls was filled with rock, and the monument was capped with an eight-inch cement lid. As an added touch, the workers wrote names on the concrete cap—not their own names, but names of the handcart people and rescuers they had come to know and love through their research and temple service.

Building the monument at Martin's Cove. Left to right: Ben Bird, Dan Barrus, Nick Hunter, Dick Hunter, Ron Broce.

The final stage of construction was to cover the walls and lids with a beautiful veneer of brown-red moss rock. Under the supervision of Bishop Lloyd Larsen, members of the stake hauled approximately twenty-eight tons of rock from La Barge, Wyoming. Bishop Larsen, his brother John, Bob Adams, Les Larsen, and many Aaronic Priesthood holders struggled to get large flatbed trucks loaded with tons of rock over Rocky Ridge. They expressed amazement at how the Willie and Martin pioneers and their rescuers had pushed and pulled handcarts and wagons loaded with precious human cargo. These men of the Riverton stake felt a sincere closeness in those hot summer days of 1992 to those who had crossed the same ground in the frozen conditions of 1856. They worked most of the day in the silence of their thoughts, interrupted occasionally by an expression of emotion, love, or thanks.

Once the rock was unloaded at the monument sites, Chuck Carper, a master brick mason from Lander, spent hundreds of hours carefully choosing and placing stones that were just right for each memorial. He brought tremendous skill and art to his craft. Brother Carper was determined that each stone used on the monuments would be perfect and would fit exactly the way it should.

On one occasion, when Brother Carper was working on the Martin's Cove monument, he set a large stone and asked Brother Don Wilson to hold it in place until the mortar dried enough to make it secure. Brother Wilson's arms soon began to tire under the weight of the stone. Brother Carper looked at him, winked, and said, "Don't let that rock slide! The Lord is watching you."

While the monuments were being constructed, another labor of love was under way to manufacture the bronze plaques that would be placed on them to describe the significance of the sites and pay tribute to the heroic pioneers of 1856. No one anticipated how difficult this part of the project would be.

In a moment of pure faith, Ron and Kim Fabrizius responded to the call of their stake president to head up the project. Brother Fabrizius had had a little previous experience with mold making and bronze casting, but he had done nothing as large and complex as the monument plaques. Besides the three main plaques, a small additional plaque was to be attached to the monument at the Willie rescue site naming those who died and were buried there, and another would be mounted near an entrance to the stake center in Riverton, giving a brief description of the entire Second Rescue effort.

In conceiving the design of the plaques, the stake presidency decided to commission a small bas-relief sculpture of a handcart scene to be placed at the top of each. They contacted artist Monte Baker, who agreed to carve a handcart scene on the bowl of a moose antler. Meanwhile, members of the stake wrote the various inscriptions and sent them for Church approval.

With the design and texts completed, it was time to begin the actual production of the plaques. Small plastic letters for use in molding the texts were located and purchased in Florida and shipped to Wyoming. The letters were expensive and were thus to be reused for each plaque.

Rich Gard built a shallow rectangular wooden box the size the plaques were to be. He and Dee Lorimer then laid out the letters and attached them to the bottom of the box. This step alone took up to nine hours for each plaque. They then installed the moose-antler artwork at the head of the text, using clay to support it.

Several tedious stages led up to the final pouring of the bronze. First, a "negative" mold was made by pouring a rubber solution into the box. After the rubber had cured, the sides of the box were removed, the rubber mold extracted, and the plastic letters picked out of the rubber. The mold, the indentation of each letter, and the original plastic letters were then cleaned by hand. As she placed, removed, and cleaned the letters again and again, Sister Lorimer's fingers bled from the use of harsh chemicals.

Next, wax had to melted and poured into the rubber mold to make a wax "positive" mold. The sisters of the Riverton Wyoming Stake cheerfully contributed more than twenty electric skillets for the melting of the wax, understanding that the skillets would be ruined for cooking purposes and would have to be thrown away.

During the summer of 1992, the Lorimer family garage, patio, and gazebo became a wax workshop. Every morning except Sunday, Luke Lorimer, age nine, would wake his seven-year-old sister, Autumn, at 5:00 A.M. While their exhausted parents caught a little sleep between "pours," these two children would dress and then kneel in prayer in the family kitchen. Luke was overheard to pray for the safety of little Autumn as they fulfilled their assignment to heat the wax in the twenty or so electric skillets.

By 6:00 the wax was all melted. At 200 degrees Fahrenheit it was a clear, red solution. The Lorimer family would carefully fill the rubber molds with wax before President Lorimer went to work. At lunchtime the rubber molds were peeled away, and Kelly Lorimer, age three, would break any faulty wax positives into pieces to be melted again. At 4:00 P.M. Luke and Autumn would again start melting wax for a 5:00 P.M. pour. The process would be repeated the next morning.

Making successful wax molds was not easy. When the first wax positive was removed from the rubber mold, there were hundreds of air bubbles trapped in the corners of the letters, a defect that, if not corrected, would lead to faulty and disfigured bronze lettering on the plaques. After spending hours fruitlessly trying to solve the problem, President Lorimer called the BYU Art Department. "They had a good laugh after I told them what we were attempting to do," he wrote later. "They told me that it was impossible to cast a plaque with sharp edges and lettering using the lost wax method." (Lorimer Personal Writings.)

Feeling somewhat desperate, the members working on the waxes finally discovered that they could remove most of the bubbles from the letters with toothpicks if they worked fast enough while the wax was still liquid. As many people as possible stood around the mold when the wax was

Clockwise, starting from left: Ron Fabrizius, President Scott Lorimer, Kelly Lorimer, Luke Lorimer, Sarah Lorimer, Jessica Lorimer, and Kami Fabrizius inspect a wax mold.

poured in. Each was assigned a particular section, and as soon as the wax was poured, they would begin popping the bubbles. Although they never were able to get an absolutely perfect cast, they were eventually able to get the problem down to no more than a few bubbles per wax positive.

Making the bronze castings for the monuments. Left to right: Doug Bauer, Charles Starks, Mike Starks.

The holes left by those few bubbles were touched up using melted wax, placed and shaped with dental tools. Sarah, Jessica, Julie, and Heika Lorimer and Kami, Lisa, and Kim Fabrizius spent hundreds of hours touching up the waxes. This valiant band of wax repairers faced challenges of aching necks, general exhaustion, and static electricity that caused the wax to literally jump off the ends of the tools onto the wax positives in the wrong places. The dental tools, however, proved to be the perfect way to touch up imperfections in the wax.

The finished wax molds were taken to Ron Fabrizius and Charles Starks's machine/welding shop for the next step, which was to use the wax positive mold to make the ceramic negative mold into which the molten bronze would ultimately be poured. Ron and Kim Fabrizius coated the wax positives with a slurry solution, allowed them to dry, and coated them again. They repeated this process over and over again until there was a half-inch ceramic shell or mold over the wax positive.

The volunteers had originally thought that the wax could be melted out of the completed ceramic molds in a kitchen oven, but the shells proved too large to fit. Brother Fabrizius came to the rescue by modifying a large oven in which he could melt the wax out of the ceramic shells.

The supreme challenge was now upon them: the pouring of the bronze plaques. In 1992 there was not a kiln or foundry in the Riverton Wyoming Stake large enough to cast plaques of this size. Three of the plaques would weigh 83 pounds each; a fourth would weigh 129 pounds with a small plaque attached. Sufficient bronze had to be melted all at once to make one complete pour.

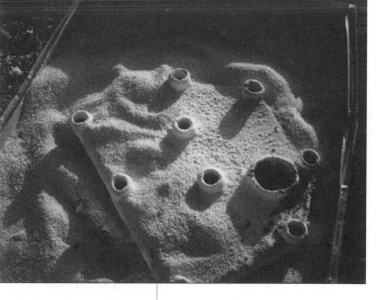

Knowing the desire of the Saints of the Riverton stake to complete this project themselves, President Lorimer asked Brother Fabrizius to construct a kiln. He willingly did so out of a 55-gallon drum lined with fire brick. He read books on how to get the proper oxygen mixture and how to have the flame swirl in the proper way around the crucible holding the bronze inside the kiln. He also manufactured large tongs to lift the crucible out of the kiln.

Ron Fabrizius then experienced eighteen straight failures in trying to pour the bronzes. Frustration aside, the whole project had begun to be very costly. Brother Fabrizius became justifiably discouraged, but he greatly desired to complete the assignment he had accepted. Seeking divine help, Ron and his wife, Kim, requested and received special priesthood blessings from the stake presidency, with President Kim McKinnon acting as voice. They were promised that they would know the techniques and processes necessary to succeed with the production of the bronze plaques. Similar blessings were given to Charles and Thelma Starks.

The ceramic shell after the bronze has been poured.

When Kim Fabrizius got to the shop on August 10, 1992, she went to her father, Charles Starks, and asked him to call the men together for a prayer before the day's casting began. He explained that some of the men were not Latter-day Saints. She said it was all right if they elected not to participate. Everyone seemed to agree that divine intervention would be needed if they were to succeed. When it was announced that they were going to pray for help with the castings, all twelve men present chose to participate in the prayer.

President Lorimer described what happened next: "The three pours were made, and all three failed. In failing, however, a pattern was noticed. A fire shield had been placed in the burnout oven that left a non-uniform temperature in the shell during wax burnout. The temperature problem caused a carbon graphite to form, causing the molten bronze to slide across the letters and not conform to the ceramic shell. The Lord showed them the error only five days before President Hinckley and hundreds of people from many states would gather at the Willie rescue site for the dedication." (Lorimer Personal Writings.)

The Lorimer family returned from the shop exhausted and discouraged. They had agreed to pour and touch up two more wax positives for each plaque. The first set of wax positives was removed from the rubber molds at 12:00 midnight. An additional set was soon poured, and the final touch-up of the first set was completed at 2:00 A.M.

Exhausted, the crew went to bed for a few hours' sleep so they could get up at 5:00 A.M. to touch up the second set of wax positives for the bronze crew to pick up at 7:00 A.M. President Lorimer knelt in prayer with his wife and pled for help. He told the Lord they had done everything they could think of, to the point of exhaustion. He prayed for the safety of the people handling the bronze. He pled with the Lord that the final casting would succeed for the benefit of his people and the fulfillment of the promises made to them. Finally he prayed that if necessary a miracle would occur, even to the point that an angel would be sent if needed to hold the plaques together as they were cast.

When President Lorimer arose at 5:00 A.M. to begin his portion of the touch-up work, he could not get his propane torch to light. He changed to a new, unused tank, but the torch would still not light. Out of exhaustion and frustration, he threw the torch against the garage wall. The instant it left his hand a thought came into his mind: "You prayed for a miracle, even an angel—where is your faith?" President Lorimer was embarrassed with his own impatience and lack of faith. He returned to the house, told his wife that they needed only one set of wax positives and that they would work this time, and left for work.

On August 13, 1992, Brother Fabrizius placed the first ceramic shell into the oven and lit the burner. The oven heated the shell to 1,800 degrees F.; it was a pure white when the door was opened, and glowed orange inside where the wax had melted out of the middle. Brother Fabrizius reached into the oven and, with only two folded asbestos cloth rags and leather gloves, picked up the ceramic mold. The mold was so hot that the leather of his gloves smoked and began shrinking the minute he touched it. He did not flinch at the heat, but carefully placed one foot in front of the other on his way to the insulated pouring bed where the molten bronze would be poured into the ceramic mold. As Brother Fabrizius carried the ceramic shell to the pouring bed, Brother Starks noticed that there was a crack all the way across its back side. (Previously Brother Fabrizius had said he would break any cracked shells to prevent possible harm to the bronze pourers.) Brother Starks yelled to Brother Fabrizius, who did not hear the caution. He laid the shell down and instructed his son Cory and another worker to lift the crucible of molten bronze out of the kiln and pour it into the shell. The bronze had been heated to 2,100 degrees F. Brother Starks yelled again not to pour the

A happy crew displays the first successful bronze plaque.

bronze, as the ceramic shell was cracked. Brother Fabrizius said, "President Lorimer said it will work. Pour the bronze." As the molten metal ran freely into the cavity of the ceramic shell, it glowed a fiery fluorescent orange through the crack. Hours passed while it cooled.

Finally the bronze was cool enough to permit the ceramic shell to be removed. Everyone waited anxiously. Brother Fabrizius carefully broke the shell away. The plaque for the Willie rescue site was beautiful—a success in every way. As in 1856 when the rescuers found the stranded travelers, a cry of joy rent the air.

The next day the plaques for the monuments at Martin's Cove, Rocky Ridge, the Riverton stake center, and the additional name plaque for the Willie rescue site monument were completed, each perfectly done on the first pour. The monuments would have first-class plaques in time for the dedication after all. Faith had been exercised, and the promises and blessings that had been given had been fulfilled.

The plaques were polished up, and volunteers spent Thursday evening and then worked through the night on Friday to grout them in place on the monuments. The crew arrived home with just enough time to clean up and, with grateful hearts, attend the dedication ceremony, knowing that the Lord's hand had been exercised forcefully in the completion of these memorials. There had been only seven hours to spare. Surely the Lord "doth nourish them, and strengthen them, and provide means whereby they can accomplish the thing which he has commanded them" (1 Nephi 17:3).

At the dedicatory service held August 15, 1992, at the Willie rescue site, President Lorimer observed:

"The monuments which we have built and which are to be dedicated today were built by craftsmen, one and all, who knew and loved these people. Nothing but the best was good enough for the Martin and Willie handcart people. We of the Riverton stake have had the opportunity to witness modern-day miracles as our faith has been tested and strengthened, and as we have participated in this wonderful project of ensuring that the pioneers' temple work is completed.

"The monuments which are being dedicated today are not monuments to those deaths which occurred here, but they are monuments to the faith of those good people. I know without a shadow of a doubt that there is life after death. As I have walked this very area, I have felt [the spirit of] Captain Willie as he returned to his people with the rescue wagons and indicated to them that they needed to send most of the wagons on to the Martin people. The exact locations of these heroic events are not known. But we know here, through spiritual confirmation, that we are very close to them.

"It has been a wonderful and special experience for us of the Riverton Wyoming Stake to gain a sure knowledge of these good people who have passed on before us but left us here with a burning testimony of the truthfulness of the gospel and the value of faith." (Meetings of the Second Rescue.)

MARY SOAR TAYLOR

Mary Soar Taylor, age thirty-one, was a widow when she came across the plains with her two sons, William Henry, twelve, and Jesse Soar Taylor, ten, in the Martin handcart company. Mary remembered their arrival in the Salt Lake Valley:

"Many had their limbs badly frozen[,] myself and William among the number. . . . I could not stand on my feet for three months after I arrived."

In Mary's letter to her posterity, she bore her testimony: "I know it is the work of God and I hope and trust that any of my posterity that may come in possession of this may be strengthened in their faith by it and be worthy of such parentage for truly we suffered much for the truth's sake but the reward of the faithful is sure."

In Kate B. Carter, "Happenings in the Valley," *Our Pioneer Heritage,* 20 vols. Salt Lake City: Daughters of Utah Pioneers, 1960, 3:247–49.

CHAPTER 12

THE SUN RANCH

*"May all who come here come with a spirit of reverence.
. . . May a spirit of solemnity rest upon them."*
PRESIDENT GORDON B. HINCKLEY

FAMILY TRADITION SAYS THAT TOM SUN WAS fourteen years old in 1860 when he probably climbed for the first time to the top of Independence Rock in central Wyoming. For a young lad with big dreams, it must have been an exciting moment.

Independence Rock is one of the most prominent natural landmarks along the Mormon/Oregon/California Trail. It occupies twenty-four acres and is 193 feet high on the north end. By the time Tom explored it for the first time, the rock already bore the names of hundreds of trappers, explorers, and pioneers who had passed this way en route to California, Oregon, and Utah. Hence, Independence Rock became known as the "Registry of the Desert."

For westward immigrants, there was no better place for celebrating the Fourth of July than Independence Rock. Patriotic significance of the date aside, they knew that reaching this landmark by early July meant they had an excellent chance of arriving at their intended destination before winter snows blanketed the peaks of the farthest western mountains. So, it was with some satisfaction that many pioneers arrived at the rock by early July, circled their wagons, made camp, and carved or scrawled their names on the surface of the huge natural landmark in black, red, or yellow paint.

From the top of this large mass of granite, Tom got his first magnificent view of the Sweetwater Valley to the west. By the time four generations of the Sun family had lived and worked there, Tom's descendants would own and manage more than one million acres of the grassy prairie land that lay in his view.

Tom Sun, whose real name was Thomas de Beau Soleil before it was Americanized, was born of French-Canadian parents in Vermont, February 28, 1846. His mother died when Tom was young, and his father remarried. Tom didn't get along very well with his new stepmother, so at age eleven he set out on his own. He headed west in search of an uncle who was thought to be in Montana. One can only imagine the dangers and hardships that faced an eleven-year-old boy making his way west, alone, in the middle of the nineteenth century.

At the Missouri River, young Tom met a French trapper named LeFever, whom everyone called "Dakota," who took the scruffy, sun-burned young man under his wing. Rather than continuing on to Montana, Tom followed Dakota for several years, fishing the rivers and learning the skills of a trapper, guide, and mountain man.

Tom Sun

Tom returned to the East long enough to participate in the Civil War, serving from the town of Manchester, Maine. Five months later he was discharged due to illness. Tom followed his dreams west again, working as a U.S. Army Indian scout and interpreter at, among other places, Fort Steele, in what would later become Carbon County, Wyoming. It was during this second journey west that Tom applied for his first water rights and established the Hub and Spoke Ranch in the shadow of Devil's Gate, three miles west of Independence Rock.

Tom Sun instilled in his family a deep love for the land they had acquired over the years, and he encouraged them to preserve it. He asked

JOHN JAQUES

John Jaques tells of camping at Independence Rock, November 1, 1856, with the Martin handcart company:

"There was a foot or eighteen inches of snow on the ground which, as there were but one or two [shovels] in camp, the emigrants had to shovel away with their frying pans, or tin plates, or anything they could use for that purpose, before they could pitch their tents. Then, the ground was frozen so hard that it was almost impossible to drive the tent pegs into it. Some of the men were so weak that it took them an hour or two to clear the places for their tents and set them up."

Stella Jaques Bell, ed., *Life History and Writings of John Jaques, including a Diary of the Martin Handcart Company*. Rexburg, Idaho: Ricks College Press, 1978.

family members never to plow up the native grass fields but rather to leave them in their natural state. Other than fence lines and changes in the river channel, the land remained for well over a century exactly as it had been when immigrants passed through on their way to California, Oregon, and Utah. The Sun family took great pride in combining a successful ranching operation with their sensitive care of the land.

Martin's Cove

Tom would soon learn that the land where he had settled in the Sweetwater Valley was the very area where three groups of Mormon pioneers—the Martin handcart company and the Hunt and Hodgett wagon trains—became stranded in early October storms of 1856 in one of the worst disasters in American westward migration. About 25 percent of the pioneers in those companies perished due to the extreme conditions. The toll would have been much higher if not for the monumental rescue effort mounted by Brigham Young and the Mormon settlers already in Salt Lake City.

More than 130 years later, interestingly enough, Tom's descendants would play a major role in enabling The Church of Jesus Christ of Latter-day Saints to officially honor those courageous handcart pioneers and their rescuers with memorials to their quest for religious freedom.

To Riverton Wyoming Stake President Scott Lorimer, an important part of the Second Rescue effort was to find a way for the Church to purchase the land made sacred by the events of 1856 for the purpose of creating official Church historical sites for the public to visit. Two sites became the focus of the Riverton stake presidency's efforts. One was Rock Creek Hollow, with its mass grave for members of the Willie handcart company. The other site was a portion of the extensive Sun Ranch. Included on this property is the place where hundreds of members of the Martin handcart company and the Hunt and Hodgett wagon trains struggled across the Sweetwater River during a bitter winter storm and sought refuge in a horseshoe-shaped ravine on the north side of the Sweetwater Valley. In that place, which later came to be known as Martin's Cove, the suffering company members camped in freezing weather with hardly any food for approximately nine days, praying for help to arrive from Salt Lake City.

At Martin's Cove monument dedication. Left to right: Kim W. McKinnon, President Gordon B. Hinckley, President R. Scott Lorimer, John Levi Kitchen, Jr.

By 1992, careful historical research had confirmed the accuracy of the location of Martin's Cove, and the Riverton Wyoming Stake presidency obtained permission from the Sun family and the Federal Bureau of Land Management (BLM) to construct a monument at the entry to the cove in memory of the pioneers and the rescue teams. The cove itself was owned by the BLM, and the Sun family owned land that was necessary to cross to gain access to the cove. The monument was dedicated on August 15, 1992, by President Gordon B. Hinckley, who at the time was a counselor in the First Presidency of the Church. On the same day he also dedicated two similar monuments about 70 miles farther west, one at the Willie rescue site near the Sweetwater River, and the other near Rocky Ridge.

As interest in these monuments and sites swelled, it soon became evident that more convenient access to Martin's Cove was desirable.

Negotiations began for the Church to acquire a portion of the Sun Ranch. Terms were finally agreed upon in April 1996.

Soon after the acquisition of the property, the Sun family's original ranch house was remodeled to become a visitors' center. Two bridges have since been built, more than 100 handcarts have been constructed for visitors' use, and the ranch has been converted into a place that the public is welcomed and encouraged to visit.

The culminating event to the years of hoping, praying, and working came on May 3, 1997, when President Gordon B. Hinckley stood on a platform under an orange canopy in front of an estimated 10,000 people on the Sun Ranch and dedicated the new Mormon Handcart Visitors' Center. In his dedicatory prayer, he expressed gratitude for the Sun family and their efforts to preserve the land through the years. Then he shared the desire that was at the heart of the project: "May all who come here come with a spirit of reverence, as they recall the experiences of their forebears. May a spirit of solemnity rest upon them. . . . May these be held scenes of remembrance and resolution as the record of the past is taught."

CHAPTER 13

VEIL CROSSING

"We will finish this bridge so no one will ever have to endure what the pioneers did. We will do it in their honor and to their memory."

CHARLES STARKS

AFTER PRESIDENT GORDON B. HINCKLEY dedicated the Mormon Handcart Visitors' Center near Devil's Gate, Wyoming, on May 3, 1997, visitors began coming by the tens of thousands. Today families, youth groups, and tourists travel from all over the United States and abroad to learn of the Mormon pioneers who suffered there. Because of the careful stewardship of four generations of the Tom Sun family, the land appears much the same as it did in pioneer times. Visitors sense the sacred spirit of this place and are humbled as they walk the paths of the early Saints.

In the fall of 1996, after final arrangements were made for the Church to purchase a portion of the Sun Ranch, local Church leaders foresaw the widespread interest that would develop in the handcart sites. Charles Starks, a member of the Riverton Wyoming Stake, remembers attending a meeting in which the future of the area was discussed: "I was overwhelmed with the impression that I was witnessing the beginning of something very great. Though the Lord had not yet revealed what would take place at the ranch, I believe we were all impressed and humbled at the tremendous potential of the entire area, from Independence Rock to Devil's Gate and Martin's Cove, and looking west toward Split Rock. . . . It is very obvious that the Lord has preserved that area to be used for his purposes in our day. This is one of the very significant locations along the Pioneer Trail, so very rich with Church history, as well as [being part of] the highway of all the migrations west in the 1800s." (Oral Interview, "The History of the Veil Bridge to Martin's Cove, Located on the Sun Ranch," pp. 2–3.)

As ideas were shared, it was clear that the land needed to be developed somewhat to accommodate visitors, and yet the environment and the spirit of the place needed to be protected and preserved. A committee was organized, and soon local Church members were working alongside employees of Church Farm Management to make improvements that would help teach and inspire the multitudes soon to come.

The Mormon Handcart Visitors' Center.

Local volunteers and Church service missionaries worked energetically on a variety of projects, including remodeling the Sun family ranch house to serve as the Mormon Handcart Visitors' Center, installing public rest rooms, leveling and grading a large parking lot, constructing 100 handcarts (designed by Bishop Mike Gard) to be made available to the public free of charge, training couple missionaries to serve as tour guides, drilling three wells, constructing campgrounds, creating a one-mile trail to Devil's Gate and a four-mile trail from the Visitors' Center to and through Martin's Cove, and making and placing trail markers.

One of the most pressing needs was for a new bridge to span the Sweetwater River near the Visitors' Center. For their ranching operations, the Sun family had used a conventional bridge supported by poles driven into the riverbed. Over time this bridge wore out and washed away during spring flooding. It was replaced in the mid-1970s by a single ninety-two-foot railroad flatcar, which was held in place by cement abutments on both sides of the Sweetwater River. That bridge was only eight and a half feet wide. In 1991, as visitors began to trickle into Martin's Cove, the Sun family was greatly concerned that someone would be hurt on the bridge or even drive off into the Sweetwater River, as the bridge had no railings and was very slippery when wet.

At the conclusion of the negotiations to buy the ranch in 1996, President Hinckley asked President Lorimer if the Riverton Wyoming Stake would be willing to either improve or replace the existing bridge. The stake presidency eagerly agreed to organize local Church members to accomplish the task. They felt strongly that the bridge should not only be able to handle significant daily traffic but also stand as a fitting and enduring memorial to the early pioneers who risked their lives wading the icy waters of the Sweetwater River in 1856.

An interesting possibility emerged early on. At the same time plans were being discussed to replace the bridge, but before any public announcement had been made, Charles Starks, a manufacturer, welder, and machinist, approached President Lorimer and asked if he needed a bridge for anything. Brother Starks explained that he had negotiated with a farmer to build a bridge for him. All the materials had been purchased when, without explanation, the farmer changed his mind. Brother Starks said he did not know whether President Lorimer needed the bridge, but that he was willing to donate it to the Church if they had a place to put it. President Lorimer said that he did indeed need a bridge, but that its design and durability would need to be certified by a civil engineer to meet code requirements. Later that evening, Brother Starks delivered already existing plans for a bridge that had been drawn several years earlier by Kent Wolz, a member of the Casper Wyoming Stake and a licensed civil engineer.

After visiting the location, Brother Wolz determined that as protection against flooding, the new bridge should be built higher above the riverbed than the former bridge had been. It was also clear from simple measure-

JOHN JAQUES

At the last crossing of the Sweetwater River, the Saints faced a stream that was cold to the point of having chunks of ice floating down it. Some women and children were helped by young men who sacrificed greatly to get them across the river. Others did the best they could on their own:

"In the rear part of the company two men were pulling one of the handcarts, assisted by one or two women, for the women pulled as well as the men all the way, so long as the hand-carts lasted. When the cart arrived at the bank of the river, one of these men, [James Bleak], who was much worn down, asked, in a plaintive tone, 'Have we got to go across there?' On being answered yes, he was so much affected that he was completely overcome. That was the last strain. His fortitude and manhood gave way. He exclaimed, 'Oh dear! I can't go through that,' and burst into tears. His wife, [Elizabeth], who was by his side, had the stouter heart of the two at that juncture, and she said soothingly, 'Don't cry, Jimmy. I'll pull the hand-cart for you.' . . . In the river the sharp cakes of floating ice below the surface of the water struck against the bare shins of the emigrant, inflicting wounds which never healed until he arrived at Salt Lake, and the dark scars of which he bears to this day."

Stella Jaques Bell, ed., *Life History and Writings of John Jaques, including a Diary of the Martin Handcart Company*. Rexburg, Idaho: Ricks College Press, 1978. The names of the man and his wife (James and Elizabeth Bleak) come from Carol Madsen, *Journey to Zion*. Salt Lake City: Deseret Book, 1997, p. 584.

ments that the bridge Brother Starks had offered was too short—it was only forty-two feet long.

After considering a variety of options, the leaders determined they would try to find an additional railroad flatcar to match the existing one. They would use cranes to place both cars higher above the riverbed on steel pilings. John Creer of Church Farm Management was able to locate a suitable railroad car that had been in an accident but was adequate for bridge building. It was purchased in Idaho and transported to Wyoming.

The beginning stages of the new bridge, built with railroad cars.

At President Lorimer's request, Bishop Lloyd Larsen agreed to serve as chairman of the project. Work on the bridge began in earnest on October 16, 1996. All labor was donated by members of the Riverton, Casper, and Rock Springs stakes.

One concern in building the bridge in the fall of the year was the danger of range fires. The autumn grasses were tall and dry, and the welders assembling the bridge were concerned that sparks could start fires and possibly burn thousands of acres. A pump was kept available at the site to put out any fires that might start.

Officials in Salt Lake City were also concerned about beginning construction so late in the year, but President Lorimer expressed his conviction that the heavy winter storms would hold off until the bridge was completed. The day before the welding was to start, the Sun Ranch was blanketed with two inches of very wet snow. John Creer commented that he thought it was not supposed to snow until the bridge was completed. President Lorimer smiled and responded that the snow was only to wet the grass and reduce the fire hazard, and that there would be no further heavy storms. That was indeed what happened. There were bitter cold temperatures and wind, but only light skiffs of snow. In contrast, neighboring Casper experienced heavy snows.

The members of the volunteer crew working on the bridge proved to be stubborn about quality. Brother Charles Starks echoed the feelings of the whole crew when he said that it was being built in memory of the Willie and Martin handcart pioneers and should therefore be as perfect as it could be.

At one point, after the two railcars had been hoisted into place by the cranes, Brother Starks had the work crews measure diagonally from all four corners to see if the railcars were squarely placed. The total diagonal length of the bridge was 92.5 feet. The bridge was found to be one-half inch out of square. Kent Wolz, the engineer, observed that since they were dealing with wrecked railcars, he was not sure they would ever get the bent steel closer to symmetry. "After all, Chuck," Brother Wolz said with a smile, "we are building a bridge, not a piano." Nonetheless, Brother Wolz, Brother Starks, and the rest of the crew were united in giving it one more try. They lifted the cars again with the cranes and carefully reset them until the diagonal measurements were accurate to within one-quarter of an inch.

Approximately eight thousand man-hours were donated to construct the bridge. The circumstances of Bishop Larsen, Brother Starks, and Brother Fabrizius permitted them to lead the labor charge by volunteering their full time and attention to the project. Out of their own pockets they were also able to pay some of their own employees to work on the bridge. In addition, there were bishops, Relief Society sisters, elders quorum presidents, Primary teachers, and stake presidency members working on and

Shirley Marsh seals the end of the planking for the bridge with the help of Judy Ramsey and Luke Lorimer.

Eliza Cusworth Burton Staker

ELIZA CUSWORTH BURTON STAKER

"Eliza [a member of the Martin hand-cart company] waded the Sweetwater River three times in one evening. First she took her [son, Joseph,] across on her back, then when she reached the other shore, she put him down, but he was frightened and tried to follow her back. She was forced to tie him to a nearby tree while she went back to get his sister. She then had to make the third trip to get her handcart. . . . Her son . . . carried the marks of their perilous journey to his grave as his foot was frozen and he lost two of his toes."

From "Eliza Cusworth Burton Staker, 1824–1914," by her daughter Eliza Jane Staker Day. Typescript in possession of Sonya Shaw, North Ogden, Utah. Photograph courtesy Esther Durfey.

around the cold steel day after day, making a bridge at the request of a prophet of God.

In the end, it was the accumulation of many "widow's mites" that built the bridge. Some were able to give more time, money, and materials than others, but each person did what he or she could according to individual circumstances. As Bishop Larsen later said, "Each contribution was a sacrifice, and each offering was equally important in the eyes of the Lord."

Relief Society sisters hauled rocks. Some brethren contributed skills or ran machinery, donating both skills and equipment. Some used precious vacation time to work on the bridge. All in all, the construction period was a time of sacrifice and joy for many, many people.

Brother Kent Wolz reported at the conclusion of the project: "I started working construction jobs forty years ago, and I have never been on one that went so smoothly as this one did. Everything was there when it needed to be there, and in the right shape. It was amazing to me." (Oral Interview, "The History of the Veil Bridge to Martin's Cove, Located on the Sun Ranch," pp. 2–3.)

Bishop Larsen saw the hand of the Lord and of the handcart people many times in enabling busy men and women to find time in their schedules to complete the volunteer project.

"All of us are private businessmen," he said. "The fact that our schedules would allow us to do the things that needed to be done to build the bridge was amazing. Ron and Chuck and I were somewhat used to having the Lord intervene and help in those situations, but Brother Wolz wasn't. [For example, we had a deadline by which we needed] to get the blueprints done. Brother Wolz called and said, "I don't think I will be able to get those blueprints to you when you need them." The blueprints were somewhat critical, so President Lorimer had all of us come to his office and we made a conference call to Brother Wolz. At one point there in the meeting, Brother Wolz said, "Say, my client has just called and postponed his project for two weeks, and I will be in good shape!" We kind of laughed and said, "That's the way the Willie people work!" (Oral Interview, "The History of the Veil Bridge to Martin's Cove, Located on the Sun Ranch," pp. 2–3.)

Brother Starks commented that through the long days working on the cold steel bridge he would see large chunks of ice floating down the Sweetwater River. His thoughts would turn to the pioneers who stood at the edge of the ice-cold Sweetwater, not wanting to cross. The memory of the suffering they endured and the courage they exhibited kept him going, he said. With great emotion he spoke his feelings: "We will finish this bridge so no one will ever have to endure what the pioneers did. We will do it in their honor and to their memory."

Bishop Lewis T. Barnett shows granite monuments placed at the ends of the Veil Crossing bridge.

In the end, those who had volunteered to build the bridge felt greatly blessed. Bishop Larsen commented: "I know that our businesses prospered during that time. The Lord really blessed us in our sacrifices. It's kind of like fast offerings. If you give those things that in reality are His, then He will bless you with more."

There were frequent discussions regarding a name for the bridge. President Lorimer hoped for a name that would honor the pioneers, their rescuers, and also those who accomplished the Second Rescue. He wanted a name that symbolized the essence of all these experiences. "Eternal Crossing," "Celestial Crossing," "Revelation Crossing," and "Temple Crossing" were suggested, but none of those possibilities seemed to contain the full message. From reflections on the significance of the work for people on both sides of the veil, the name "Veil Crossing" emerged. The

SARAH ANN FRANKS

This incident most likely took place in Martin's Cove:

"Sarah [Ann Franks, member of the Martin handcart company] became so weak and ill with chills and fever that she was taken into one of the wagons. Her sweetheart [George Padley] also became very ill from hunger and exposure and developed peneumonia and died. Sarah took her long-fringed shawl from her almost freezing body and had the brethren wrap her sweetheart's body in it. She couldn't bear to think of his being buried with nothing to protect him from shoveled dirt and ravages of the weather. It has been said that the weather was so severe that his body was hung from a tree for others, who followed, to bury. [This also spared his body from being ravaged by wolves.] Sarah was too ill to even raise her head and witness the arrival of the relief wagons, which were greeted with joy and thanksgiving. . . . The sick were made comfortable in the wagons and were sent on ahead of the main company to the Salt Lake Valley."

"Descendants of Thomas Mackay—Utah Pioneer, Vol. 1, Wives and Children." Published by Thomas Mackay Family Organization, Murray, Utah, 1964.

Spirit testified that this name fully symbolized what had truly happened on the high plains of Wyoming, then and now.

Two large granite monuments, quarried in St. Cloud, Minnesota, were shipped to Riverton. They were carved by Bishop Lewis Barnett and then placed at the bridge, one at each end, as gifts from the members of the Riverton Wyoming Stake. The granite boulder on the south end of the bridge, which leads north toward Martin's Cove, is carved with the words:

VEIL

CROSSING

RESCUE OF

1856

The granite boulder on the north end of the bridge, which leads back to the Mormon Handcart Visitors' Center, reads:

VEIL

CROSSING

SECOND RESCUE

1992

On July 26, 1997, the Riverton Wyoming Stake held a Pioneer Day celebration at Veil Crossing, at which time the two stone monuments placed at the bridge as well as the granite monument at Rock Creek Hollow were dedicated by President John Levi Kitchen, Jr., first counselor in the stake presidency.

President R. Scott Lorimer observed on that joyful occasion: "These stones that we, the people of the Second Rescue, have placed at Veil Crossing are a reminder to us and all who pass this way, that there once was a time when we entered into a covenant with the Lord regarding those who passed here many years ago. Because of that covenant we [and they] were in a very literal sense allowed to reach across the veil and touch each other. The blessings on both sides are full, and the balance is equally laden with understanding, joy, peace, and love. May we never forget what we know. May we never forget our covenants. May we never stray from our eternal promise to so live that we [and they] may one day see each other clearly." (Meetings of the Second Rescue.)

By the end of summer 1997, more than seventy thousand visitors had walked the trail over Veil Crossing, many pulling handcarts. Some absorbed the drama and hardships of the handcart and wagon train people who suffered there. Others who crossed the bridge explored in their minds for the first time the very idea of a veil between this life and the next. Still others were pilgrims reflecting on the thinness of that veil and contemplating other veil crossings, past and future. In any case, the meaning of the bridge is profound, and the Spirit is strong at Veil Crossing.

In his dedicatory prayer, President Kitchen summed up the feelings of many stake members as he looked back on the privilege that had been theirs to participate in a project of such far-reaching and eternal proportions:

"We . . . pronounce a benediction on the Second Rescue as we have known it. For now it has gone beyond the boundaries of our stake and will continue to grow and spread across the earth. Many will be involved and many will be blessed as their lives are touched, as our lives have been touched through the spirit of the Second Rescue.

"Much work yet is needed by our stake to help, not only with the logistical needs of seeing this work go forward, but also in completion of the research and temple ordinances for the Hunt and Hodgett wagon trains and whatever else we are called upon to do by those who will carry the torch forward from this point. We, the people of the Second Rescue, are grateful for the opportunity we have had to serve and are willing to continue to serve in whatever we are asked to do."

EPILOGUE TO THE SECOND RESCUE

BY PRESIDENT ROBERT SCOTT LORIMER

As WORD-OF-MOUTH VERSIONS CIRCULATE regarding occurrences in the Riverton Wyoming Stake, the question is increasingly asked, "What was the Second Rescue?" Others want to know, "Is it still going on? Was it about land acquisitions along the Mormon Trail? Was it simply a program developed to get a stake enthused about family history and temple work? Can we come see it or be part of it? Can we do something similar?"

The simple truth of the matter is that the Second Rescue was not a program in any sense of the word. It was a direct revelation to a stake president concerning temple ordinances that needed to be completed for members of the Willie and Martin handcart companies and faithful stake members who willingly sacrificed so this and other work would be completed. Included in the totality of the Second Rescue were more than 4,200 temple ordinances completed for the Willie and Martin pioneers in the Ogden Temple, the construction of three monuments in memory of the handcart companies, several blessings given to the members of the Riverton Wyoming Stake by their Church leaders, three dedicatory services under the direction of President Gordon B. Hinckley, and the purchase of large tracts of land at the Willie and Martin sites.

These events have led to the development of a visitors' center in central Wyoming that will allow thousands of people to visit firsthand the pioneer past of The Church of Jesus Christ of Latter-day Saints. The lands that were purchased have been preserved over the years by faithful stewards and remain substantially as they were when the pioneers made their westward migration. Thousands will renew their pioneer heritage, and many others will feel the spirit of pioneer commitment and be introduced to the true gospel of Jesus Christ.

Visitors will leave these historical sites with a desire to return to where the Second Rescue began. They will learn of the value of eternal families and how to have such through the sealing keys restored in this dispensation through the Prophet Joseph Smith Jr. Their hearts will be turned to their progenitors as well as their posterity, desiring what the Willie and Martin pioneers desired, to live together forever as families in the presence of God.

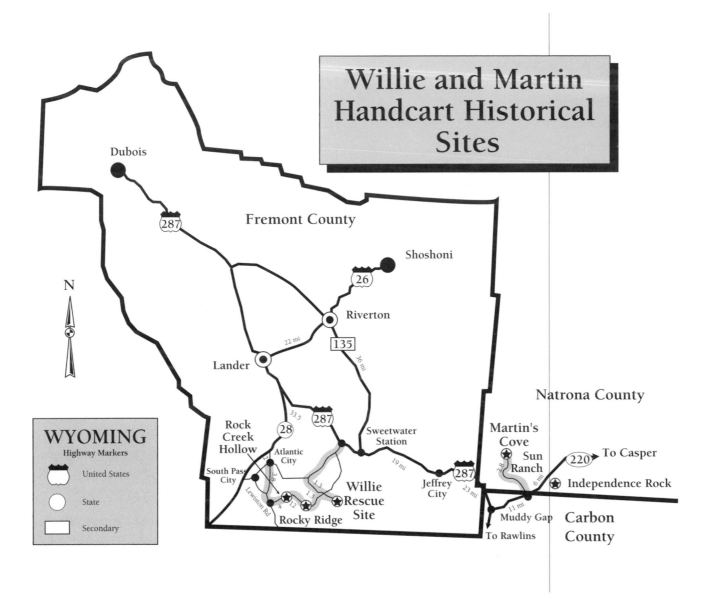

Willie and Martin Handcart Historical Sites

Dubois

Fremont County

287

N

Shoshoni

26

Riverton

22 mi

Lander

135

36 mi

Natrona County

33.5

Rock
Creek
Hollow

28

287

Sweetwater
Station

Martin's
Cove

Sun
Ranch

220 → To Casper

WYOMING

Highway Markers

Atlantic
City

19 mi

2.8

South Pass
City

United States

State

Secondary

3.8

1.3

287

6 mi

Independence Rock

Willie
Rescue
Site

Jeffrey
City

23 mi

Lewiston Rd.

4

12

1.3

11 mi

Rocky Ridge

Muddy Gap

Carbon
County

To Rawlins

ROSTERS OF THE PIONEER COMPANIES AND RESCUERS

WILLIE HANDCART COMPANY

The following names, ages in May of 1856, and birthplaces have been taken from Leroy R. Hafen and Ann W. Hafen, Handcarts to Zion, 1856–1860 (Glendale, Calif.: The Arthur H. Clark Co., 1960), pp. 289–94; Journal History of The Church of Jesus Christ of Latter-day Saints (Archives, LDS Church Historical Department, Salt Lake City, Utah), 11/9/1856; and Susan Easton Black, Membership of The Church of Jesus Christ of Latter-day Saints, 1830–1848 (Provo, Utah: Brigham Young University Religious Studies Center, 1989), pp. 1–41. Discrepancies and names from other sources are also listed. In this and all other lists, birth and death dates are in 1856 unless specified otherwise.

From Florence, Nebraska, to Salt Lake City, Utah, and those who died previously:

Ahmanson, John (or Johan A.) (28), birthplace Sweden
Andersen, Metta Marie (19), sister, birthplace Denmark
Andersen, Anne Marie (16), sister, birthplace Denmark
Andersen, Christena (14), sister, birthplace Denmark
Anderson, Anne (or Johanna C.) (29), birthplace Denmark
Anderson, Christina, Independent Wagons
Anderson, David (17), birthplace England
Anderson, Marie (or Maria K.) (54), birthplace Denmark
Anderson, Nils (or Niels) (41),

birthplace Denmark, died October 24 and was buried at Rock Creek
Anderson, Mette (or Metta) (49), wife, birthplace Denmark
Anderson, Anna (14), daughter, birthplace Denmark
Anderson, Anders (8)
Atwood, Millen (38), birthplace Connecticut
Bailey, John (51), and family, birthplace England, died en route
Bailey, Elizabeth (51 or 52), wife, birthplace England, died October 24 and was buried at Rock Creek
Bailey, Elizabeth (17), birthplace England
Bayliss, stillborn girl, daughter of

Hannah Bayliss, born on ship *Thornton*
Bird, Mary Ann Fern (39), and family, birthplace England
Bird, Ezra (14), birthplace England
Bird, Martha Ann (12), birthplace England
Bird, Sarah (10)
Bird, Susannah (8), birthplace England
Bird, William Fred (6), birthplace England
Bodenham, Thomas (1), son of Mary Bodenham, died on ship *Thornton*
Bowington (or Boyington), Thomas (26), with Perpetual Emigration Fund wagons
Bowles, Edward (50), and family, birthplace England

Bowles, Ann (52), wife, birthplace England

Bowles, Thomas (19), birthplace England

Bowles, Enoch (11), birthplace England

Brazier, George (21), brother, birthplace England. Name also listed in *Journal History*, 11/9/1856, with the words "and Jane"

Brazier, John (19), brother, birthplace England. Name not listed in *Journal History*, 11/9/1856, but a Jane Brazier is listed with George Brazier

Bretton (or Brittian or Britton), Mary E. (or Mary Ann) (51 or 55), birthplace England

Browant (or Browand or Bravandt), Emma (or Emelia) (18), birthplace Denmark

Brown, Castina (or Christina) (26), stayed at Fort Laramie

Brown, Ellen Ward (44), and family

Brown, John

Brown, William

Brown, Elizabeth

Brown, Sarah

Brown, James

Brown, Ann

Brown, Frances

Bryant, Ann (69), birthplace England, died September 26 between Chimney Rock and Scottsbluff, Nebraska

Burt, Alexander (19), birthplace Scotland

Burton, Eliza Cusworth (32), and family

Burton, Joseph (7)

Burton, Martha (4)

Calchwell, Mary A., and family

Caldwell, Margaret Ann (40), and family

Caldwell, Robert (17)

Caldwell, Thomas (14)

Caldwell, Elizabeth (12)

Caldwell, Agnes (9)

Campkin, Martha Webb (35), and family, birthplace England

Campkin, Wilford George (8), birthplace England

Campkin, Francessa (or Frencessa) (5), birthplace England

Campkin, Harriet (4), birthplace England

Campkin, Martha Ann (2), birthplace England

Campkin, Isaac James (7 months), birthplace England

Cantwell, James Sherlock, Independent Wagons. He and his family were with the Willie company until Fort Laramie, where they waited and joined the Hodgett company because of a lack of stock for their wagons

Cantwell, Elizabeth, Sr.

Cantwell, Francis R. (17)

Cantwell, James

Cantwell, William

Cantwell, Ellen (7)

Cantwell, Mary Ann

Cantwell, Elizabeth, Jr

Charles (or Choales), Sarah (24)

Chetwin, Martha (or Maria) (21)

Child (no name given), died July 1 at Iowa City camp

Chislett, John (24), birthplace England

Christensen (or Christenson), Anders (21)

Christiansen, Niel (or Niels) Lars, with Independent Wagons, interpreter and counselor to Danish Saints

Cook, Minea (or Minnie Ann) (35), birthplace England

Cook, Sophia, with daughter

Cooper, Ann (36), and family, birthplace England

Cooper, Mary Ann (6), birthplace England

Cooper, Adelaide (4), birthplace England

Cooper, Sarah Ann (2), birthplace England, died July 5 at Iowa City camp

Cox (or Copp or Coop or Cope), Theophilus William (25), birthplace England, died November 7

Crook, Sophia Mason (65), and daughter, birthplace England

Crook, Eliza (19), birthplace England

Culley, Benjamin (60), father, birthplace England, died October 4

Culley, Elizabeth (20 or 23), daughter, birthplace England

Culley, Jane (22 or 25), daughter, birthplace England

Culwell, Robert, broke collarbone milking a cow on August 30

Cunningham, James (54), and family, birthplace Scotland

Cunningham, Elizabeth Nicholson (48), wife, birthplace Scotland

Cunningham, Catherine (17), birthplace Scotland

Cunningham, George (15), birthplace Scotland

Cunningham, Elizabeth (12), birthplace Scotland

Cunningham, Margaret (9), birthplace Scotland

Curtis, George (64), birthplace England, died October 16 on the Sweetwater

Curtis, Rachel (75), died on ship *Thornton*

Dalglish (or Daglish or Douglish), Margaret (29)

Danish Child (no name listed) died June 24 at Pond Creek

Davenport, Lucinda, left company on October 9 at Fort Laramie

Davenport, Melissa, with Independent Wagons, joined Hodgett company at Fort Laramie

Dorney, Mary Davis (64), mother, birthplace England

Dorney, Hannah (25), daughter, birthplace England

Dorney, Lott, son

Edwick, William (17), returned to Fort Laramie on October 12

Elder, Joseph Benson (21), birthplace Indiana

Evans, Amelia (18)

Fannel (or Funnell), Mary A. Winters (62), mother

Fannel, Elizabeth (20 or 22), daughter

Findlay, Allen M. (or Allan) (26), and family, birthplace Scotland

Findlay, Jessie Ireland (26), wife, married on ship *Thornton*

Findlay, Mary McPherson (59), mother

Forbes, Elizabeth (8), birthplace Scotland, with Isabelle Wilkie, widow

Gadd, Samuel (40 or 42), and family, birthplace England, died October 9

Gadd, Eliza Chapman (40 or 41), wife, birthplace England

Gadd, Alfred (18), birthplace England

Gadd, Jane, (16), birthplace England

Gadd, William Chapman (11 or 12), birthplace England

Gadd, Samuel (10 or 11), birthplace England, died October 24 and was buried at Rock Creek

Gadd, Mary Ann (7), birthplace England

Gadd, Sarah (5), birthplace England

Gadd, Isaac (1), twin, birthplace England

Gadd, Daniel (1), twin, birthplace England, died October 4

Gardner, James (27), and family, birthplace England

Gardner, Hannah Gubbins (27), wife, birthplace England

Gardner, Mary Ann (6), birthplace England

Gardner, Agnes E. (5), birthplace England

Gardner, Frederick J. (3 or 2), birthplace England

Gardner, John W. (7 or 11 months), birthplace England

Geary, John Thomas, with Independent Wagons, joined Hodgett company at Fort Laramie

Geary, Sophia, with Independent Wagons

Geary, Sophia Ann, with Independent Wagons

Gibb (or Gibbs), James (61 or 67), and wife, died October 23 and was buried at Rock Creek

Gibb, Mary (53), wife

Gilby, Ann B., and sons

Gilby, Matthew (8)

Gilby, Frances W. (10)

Gillman, Chesterton John (64 or 66 or 47), birthplace England, died October 23 and was buried at Rock Creek

Girdlestone (or Gurdlestone or Gridlestone), Thomas (62 or 63), and family, died October 25

Girdlestone (or Gurdlestone), Mary Betts (59), wife, birthplace England, died October 30 and was buried near the Green River

Girdlestone, Emma (21), daughter, birthplace England

Godfrey, Ann Herbert (23), birthplace England, married by Bishop Taylor in Iowa City on July 15

Godfrey, Richard (21), birthplace England

Gregerson (or Gregeson), Marcan (or Maren) (26)

Griffiths, Catherine M. (32)

Griffiths, Edward (25), birthplace Wales

Griffiths, Mary P. (28)

Groves, William (22), birthplace England, died October 25 and was buried at Rock Creek

Gurney (or Gumer or Gunrer), Charles (36), and family

Gurney, Charlotte (37), wife

Gurney, Mary A. (15)

Gurney, Joseph (13)

Hailey (or Haley), William (66), with wife, died September 13 at North Bluff Fork

Hailey, Catherine (63)

Hansen, Maren (or Mary Ann) (52), died August 14 and was buried at Florence

Hanson, Cassius

Hanson, Nils (or Niels) (43), husband

Hanson, Anna Catherine (42), wife

Hanson (or Hansen), Rasmus Peter (40), husband, died October 19 on the Sweetwater

Hanson, Anna (40), wife

Hanson (or Hansen), Rasmus Peter (16), son, died November 6 on the Weber River

Hardwick, Richard (50 or 63), died October 21 on the Sweetwater

Henderson, James (27), from Scotland, died October 18 on the Sweetwater

Henderson, Jane (26)

Henderson, James, infant

Herbert, Anna (or Ann or Hannah) (26 or 16), mother

Herbert, Charles (2 yrs., 11 mo.), son

Hill, Emily (20), sister, birthplace England, became E. H. Woodmansee, poetess

Hill, Julia (22 or 23), sister, birthplace England, became wife of Israel Ivins

Hill, John, husband

Hill, Sarah D., wife

Hodges, Janet (Janetta) (55)

Hodges, Mary (20)

Hooley (or Holley), Thomas (20 or 21), birthplace England

Howard, Ann (30)

Humphries, George (45), and family, birthplace England

Humphries, Harriet Harding (46 or 47), wife, birthplace England

Humphries, Edwin (17 or 18), birthplace England

Humphries, Ann (16), birthplace England

Humphries, Mary (14 or 15), birthplace England

Humphries, Elizabeth (12), birthplace England

Humphries, Hannah (9), birthplace England

Humphries, Selina (or Celena) (6), birthplace England

Humphries, James (1), birthplace England

Hurren (or Harren), James (29), and family

Hurren, Eliza (or Mary) Reeder (26), wife, and daughter of David Reeder, also in Willie company

Hurren, Mary (7)

Hurren, Emma (4)

Hurren, Sarah (2)

Hurren, Selena (or Seleam or Selina), born July 14 or 15 at Iowa City, died July 28 or 30 at Cherry Creek, along the trail in Iowa

Impey (or Empey), Jesse (31), and family, birthplace England, died September 22

Impey, Mary A. Folks (or Folkes) (29), wife, birthplace England

Impey, William (9), birthplace England,

died November 7 in cottonwood grove near East Canyon Creek

Impey, James (6), birthplace England

Impey, Ann (4), birthplace England

Impey, Sarah J. (9 months), birthplace England

Ingra, George (68), and wife, from England, died October 4

Ingra, Elizabeth (75), wife, birthplace England, died September 3, a little way past Buffalo Creek

Jacobson, Paul (53 or 55), and family, from Denmark, died October 13

Jacobson, Lovisa (or Luisa) (53), wife

Jacobson, Peter (24 or 29), and family

Jacobson, Anna K. (32), wife

Jacobson, Jens Peter (3), son

James, John (52 or 53 or 61), birthplace Wales, died October 27 on the Sweetwater

James, William (38 or 46), and family, birthplace England, died October 24 and was buried at Rock Creek

James, Jane (40 or 41), wife, birthplace England

James, Sarah (19), birthplace England

James, Emma Jane (15 or 16), birthplace England

James, Reuben (13 or 14), birthplace England

James, Mary Ann (11), birthplace England

James, Martha (9), birthplace England

James, George (6), birthplace England

James, John Parley (3 or 5), birthplace England

James, Jane (6 or 8 months), birthplace England, died on ship *Thornton*

Janes (or Jensen), Petrina C. (25)

Jeffry (or Jefferies or Jeffrey), William (24)

Jensen, Catherine (24 or 18)

Jensen, Johanna Marie (21)

Jensen, Jens C. (2), from Denmark, died June 30 at Iowa City camp

Jenson, Andreas (or Andres or Anders) (47 or 49), and family, birthplace Denmark, died October 29 on the Big Sandy

Jenson, Anna Christensen (47), wife

Jenson, Michael (10), birthplace Denmark

Jenson, Anton (8), birthplace Denmark

Jenson, Carsten

Jones, Ellen (6), with John Bailey

Jorgensen (or Jergenson), Anders (or Andrew) (44 or 46), and family, birthplace Denmark

Jorgensen, Elizabeth Nielsen (42), wife, birthplace Denmark

Jorgensen, Hans (12), birthplace Denmark

Jorgensen (or Jergonson), Maren (or Mareann) (8 or 9), birthplace Denmark

Jorgensen, Anna (or Ane), birthplace Denmark

Jorgensen, Jorgen (3), birthplace Denmark

Jorgensen (or Jergonson), Christian (or Christen or Christine)

Jorgensen, Maren (or Maria) S. (8), birthplace Denmark, died November 7 near East Canyon Creek

Jost, John A., with Independent Wagons, joined Hodgett company at Fort Laramie

Jost, Maryann (or Mary Ann), Sr., with Independent Wagons

Jost, Catherine Ann, with Independent Wagons

Jost, Samuel, with Independent Wagons

Jost, Thomas, with Independent Wagons

Jost, Maryann (or Mary Ann), Jr., with Independent Wagons

Jost, Andrew James, with Independent Wagons

Kay (or Key), Rose (50), and family

Kay, Margaret (3), daughter of James and Mary Kay, died on ship *Thornton*

Kelley, Barbara (29)

Kelly, John (31), and family, birthplace England

Kelly, Mary Carmichael (30), wife

Kelly, John C. (2 or 7), birthplace England

Kirby, Anna (or Hannah) (34)

Kirby, Mary (or Maria) (14)

Kirkpatrick, Elizabeth (31)

Kirkwood, Margaret C. (47), and family, from Scotland

Kirkwood, Robert (22), son, from Scotland

Kirkwood, Thomas (19), son, from Scotland

Kirkwood, James (11), son, from Scotland, died October 24 at Rock Creek

Kirkwood, Joseph (4)

Knutsen, Kersten (60), birthplace Denmark, died October 29 on the Big Sandy

Laird, James (30 or 32), and family, birthplace Ireland

Laird, Mary Rennie (or Rainey) (29), birthplace Scotland

Laird, Joseph Smith (6), birthplace Scotland

Laird, Edward (4), birthplace Scotland

Laird, Elizabeth (1), birthplace Scotland

Langman, Rebecca (20 or 22), birthplace England

Lark, Mary F. (10), daughter of William and Mary Lark, died on ship *Thornton*

Larson (or Larsen), Peter (43), and family, from Denmark, died October 3, twenty-one miles west of Fort Laramie

Larson, Anna Christine (37), wife

Larson, Niels (12)

Larson (or Larsen), Anna Sophie (or Sophia) (10 or 11), birthplace, Denmark, died October 21 on the Sweetwater

Larson, Martine (or Martin) (5)

Larson, Lars Julius, born July 5 at Iowa City camp, died October 16 on the Sweetwater

Leatham, James (or Jeemie) (17), husband

Leatham, Margaret Irvine (16), wife

Ledingham (or Ledington), William (30), and family

Ledingham, Catron (or Catherine) (29 or 32), wife

Ledingham, Alexander (6)

Ledingham, William (5)

Ledingham, Robert McK. (3)

Ledingham, Mary (1), from Scotland, died July 7 at Iowa City camp

Leeson, Ruvina, with Independent Wagons, joined Hodgett company at Fort Laramie

Leeson (or Leason), William N. (2), from U.S., with Independent Wagons, died September 28 of canker in the stomach

Linford, John (47 or 49), and family, birthplace England, died October 21 on the Sweetwater

Linford, Maria (42 or 43), wife, birthplace England

Linford, George J. (17), birthplace England

Linford, Joseph W. (14), birthplace England

Linford, Amasa C. (11), birthplace England

Loutross, Louisa (or Louiza or Marian) (30)

Madsen, Ole, Sr.

Madsen, Ole (41), and family, birthplace Denmark, died October 24 and was buried at Rock Creek

Madsen, Anna (or Ane) Nielsen (44 or 46), wife

Madsen (or Olsen), Johanna M. (or Hannah or Johanne Maria) (15 or 16), birthplace Denmark

Madsen (or Olsen), Metta Kirstine (or Christena or Stena) (13)

Madsen (or Olsen), Anna Marie (or Anne Marie or Maria) (10), birthplace Denmark

Madsen (or Olsen), Anders (or Andrew) (5 or 6)

Madsen, Peter (49), from Jutland, Denmark, died November 2 near Fort Bridger

Madsen, Metta Marie Nielson (45)

Madsen, Peter (62 or 66), from Copenhagen, Denmark, died November 5 in Echo Canyon

Madsen, Petrea (36), daughter

Marrott, William (34)

Marsen, Peter, and family

McCullick (or McCullock or McCollick), John (20)

McKey (or McKay), Joseph (57), birthplace Ireland

McNeil, Christina (24)

McPhail (or McPhell or McPhael or McPhiel), Archibald (30 or 40), and family, birthplace Scotland, died November 6 in Echo Canyon

McPhail, Jane McKinnon (33 or 36), wife, birthplace Scotland

McPhail, Henrietta (15), birthplace Scotland

McPhail, Sarah (4)

McPhail, Jane (3), birthplace Scotland

McPhail, Donald, on ship *Thornton*'s list

Meadows, Joseph (32), with wife, birthplace England

Meadows, Amelia Pendrick (33)

Millard, Esther (31 or 33), birthplace England

Miller, Mary A. (30)

Miller, Mercy (26), and son

Miller, William A. S. (5)

Mortensen, Bodil (9), traveling with Jens Nielson family, died October 24 and was buried at Rock Creek

Mortenson, Peter (50), and family, birthplace Denmark

Mortensen (or Mortenson), Lena (or Helena) Sanderson (47 or 48), wife, birthplace Denmark

Mortensen (or Peterson), Anna (or Annie) Kirstine (24), birthplace Denmark

Mortensen (or Peterson), Anders Jorgen (22), birthplace Denmark

Mortensen (or Peterson), Hans Jorgen (18), birthplace Denmark

Mortensen (or Peterson), Lars (13), birthplace Denmark

Mortensen (or Peterson), Metta Kirstine (10 or 11), birthplace Denmark

Mortensen (or Peterson), Maria (or Mary J.) (8), birthplace Denmark

Mortensen (or Peterson), Caroline (5 or 6)

Moulton, Thomas (45 or 55), and family, birthplace England

Moulton, Sarah Denton (37 or 38), wife, birthplace England

Moulton, Sarah (19), birthplace England

Moulton, Mary Ann (14 or 15), birthplace England

Moulton, William (12), birthplace England

Moulton, Joseph (10), birthplace England

Moulton, James (7), birthplace England

Moulton, Charlotte (4), birthplace England

Moulton, Sophia (2), birthplace England

Moulton, Charles Alma, born on ship *Thornton*

Neilsen (or Nielson or Nilson or Anderson), Ella (or Helle or Lolly) (22), died October 24 and was buried at Rock Creek

Neilson, Ole, and family

Neilson, Sister, wife

Neilson, Hans Jorgon

Neilson, Wilhelmina Kristine

Neilson, Fredrich Ferdinand

Neilson, Dorothea Olevia

Neilson, Ludvig B.

Newman, Mary Ann (37), and children

Newman, Eliza (or Elizabeth) (14 or 17), birthplace England

Newman, William (14), birthplace England

Newman, John (12), birthplace England

Newman, Mary Ann (2 or 9), birthplace England

Newman, Caroline (2 or 7), birthplace England

Newman, Ellen (5), birthplace England

Nielsen, Bertha

Nielson (or Nielsen), Jens (35 or 40), and family, birthplace Denmark

Nielson, Elsie (or Else) (26 or 43), wife, birthplace Denmark

Nielson, Niels (or Jens) (5 or 6), son, died October 24 and was buried at Rock Creek

Nockolds (or Nockles or Kockles or Knockles or Nockholds), John (60 or 66), from England, died October 19 on the Sweetwater

Norris, Cecelia (or Celia) (26), birthplace England

Norris, Sarah (or Ann) (22), birthplace England

Oakey, Thomas (42), and family, birthplace England

Oakey, Ann Collett (43), wife, birthplace England

Oakey, Ann (23), birthplace England

Oakey, Charles (18), birthplace England

Oakey, Jane (16), birthplace England

Oakey, Heber S. (or Heber Thomas) (14), birthplace England

Oakey, Lorenzo N. (or Lorenzo Moroni) (12), birthplace England

Oakey, Rhoda Rebecca (10 or 11), birthplace England, died November 9 near Little Mountain

Oakey, Reuben Hyrum (8), birthplace England

Oakey, Sarah Ann (4), birthplace England

Oborn (or Osborn), Joseph (43 or 44), and family, birthplace England, died October 30 on the Green River

Oborn, Maria Stradling (45), wife, birthplace England

Oborn, John (12), birthplace England

Oliver, Ann (23)

Oliver, James (31 or 33), birthplace England

Oliver, Charles, with Perpetual Emigration Fund Wagons

Olsen, Ann (or Anne) (46 or 64), from Denmark, died October 24 and was buried at Rock Creek

Olsen, Lorenzo N. (12), son

Ore, Abraham (40 or 42), and wife, birthplace England

Ore, Eliza (41 or 42), wife, birthplace England

Osborn, Ann (23 or 24), birthplace England

Osborne (or Osborn), Daniel (35), and family, died November 1, fifteen miles west of the Green River

Osborne, Susannah Rebecca Tillet (33), wife, died November 5 in Echo Canyon

Osborne, Susannah (10), birthplace England

Osborne (or Osborn), Daniel (7), birthplace England, died October 19 on the Sweetwater

Osborne, Sarah Ann (3), birthplace England

Osborne, Martha Ann (1), birthplace England

Page, William (17 or 19), birthplace England

Panting, Elizabeth Crook (26 or 27 or 28), and family, birthplace England

Panting, Christopher (5), birthplace England

Panting, Jane (9 months or 1 year), birthplace England

Peacock, Alfred (18 or 19), birthplace England, left company on October 12, and returned to Fort Laramie

Perkins, Mary Ann (59 or 62 or 64), birthplace England, died October 21 on the Sweetwater

Peterson, Christian Sorensen (9), traveling alone

Peterson, Jens (36), and family, birthplace Denmark

Peterson, Anna (or Ane) Jensen (32 or 33), wife, birthplace Denmark

Peterson, Johanna (or Sophia) (12), birthplace Denmark

Peterson, Metta Maria (or Mette) (10), birthplace Denmark

Peterson, Hans Peter (7), birthplace Denmark

Peterson, Christian (or Kristen) (5), birthplace Denmark

Peterson, Peter (4), birthplace Denmark

Peterson, James Christian (11 months or 1 year), birthplace Denmark

Peterson, Sophie (or Catherine Wilhelmine) (31), and family

Peterson, Peter (10)

Peterson, Thomas (7), fell through hatchway on ship *Thornton* and died

Peterson, Emma Sophie (5)

Peterson, Anna Johanne (3)

Peterson, Otto August (1)

Phillpot (or Philpot), William (51), and family, birthplace England, died October 17 on the Sweetwater

Phillpot (or Philpot), Eliza (36), wife, from England, died October 22 on the Sweetwater

Phillpot, Julia M. (13), birthplace England

Phillpot, Martha Eliza (11), birthplace England

Pilgrim, Rebecca (30), birthplace England

Rasmussen, Rasmine, died on ship *Thornton* of inflammation of the brain

Read, James (21), and family

Reade, Sister, Alma Babbitt left her with the company

Reed (or Read), William (62 or 63), and family, birthplace England, died October 1, just past Fort Laramie

Reed, Sarah (62 or 64), wife

Reed, Naomi

Reed, Joseph C. (14), birthplace England

Reeder (or Reader), David (54), and family, birthplace England, died October 1, just past Fort Laramie

Reeder, Robert (19), birthplace England

Reeder (or Reader), Caroline (16 or 17), birthplace England, died October 15, one mile past Independence Rock

Richins (or Richens), John (22), and family, birthplace England

Richins, Charlotte (21), wife, birthplace England

Richins, Hannah Louiza (1), birthplace England, died July 12 or 13 at Iowa City camp

Richins, Franklin Thorton, born July 15 at Iowa City camp

Roberts, John (41 or 42), birthplace England, died October 16 on the Sweetwater

Roberts, Mary (44), birthplace England, died October 26, fifteen miles west of Rock Creek

Rogers, Jemima (23), and daughter, birthplace England

Rogers, Elizabeth (8), daughter, birthplace England

Rowley, Ann Jewell (46 or 48), and family, birthplace England

Rowley, Louisa (18), birthplace England

Rowley, Elizabeth (16 or 17), birthplace England

Rowley, John (14), birthplace England

Rowley, Samuel (12 or 13), birthplace England

Rowley, Richard (11 or 12), birthplace England

Rowley, Thomas (10), birthplace England

Rowley, Jane (7), birthplace England

Rowley, Eliza (or Ann) (28 or 30), step-daughter, birthplace England, died October 19 on the Sweetwater

Rowley, Jane (26), birthplace England

Sandberg (or Sanberk), Jens Truedson (37 or 38), birthplace Sweden

Savage, Levi (36), birthplace Ohio

Season, Sister

Season, Boy (2), died September 21

Showell, Harriet (30 or 31), sister, birthplace England

Showell, Ellen C. (14), sister

Siler, Andrew L., Captain, and company, in charge of four Independent Wagons in Willie company; left Willie company at Fort Laramie to join Hodgett company because of lack of stock

Sister (no name listed), died July 9 at Iowa City camp

Smith, Andrew (19), birthplace Scotland

Smith, Margery (or Margerie) (51), and family, birthplace Scotland

Smith, Margery (or May) (22), birthplace Scotland

Smith, Jane (17)

Smith, Mary (15)

Smith, Elizabeth (13)

Smith, Alexander J. (6)

Smith, William (47 or 48), and wife, birthplace England, died October 25 past Rock Creek

Smith, Eliza (40), wife, birthplace England, died October 19 on the Sweetwater

Stanley, Betsey (or Elizabeth) (38 or 39), birthplace England

Steed, Sarah (20)

Stewart, Jane Ann (26), single

Stewart, Nancy, was traveling with Almon Babbitt and joined Willie company on August 31 as a passenger in James Cantwell's Independent Wagon; joined Hodgett company at Fort Laramie

Stewart, Thomas (38), and family

Stewart, Margaret (44), wife, birthplace Scotland, died en route

Stewart, William (12)

Stewart, Ann B. (10)

Stewart, Thomas (8)

Stewart, John (4)

Stockdale, Mary A. (or Marianne) (18)

Stone, Susannah (or Susan) (25), birthplace EnglandStuart, Jane A.

Stuart (or Stewart), John (31 or 32), and family, birthplace Scotland

Stuart, Ann Waddle (29 or 30), wife, birthplace Scotland

Stuart, John (6), birthplace Scotland

Stuart, Mary (or Margaret Ann) (2 months), birthplace Scotland

Summers, Elizabeth (27)

Summers, Emma (27)

Tait (or Taite), Ann (or Anna F.) (31), birthplace Scotland, died October 20

Tassell, Kitty Ann (or Kate Ann) (28 or 38)

Tesit, Ann, sister

Tesit (or Teait), Elizabeth, sister

Tait, Elizabeth (25)

Tealt, Elizabeth

Tite, Elizabeth (25), birthplace England

Toffield, Ellen (43)

Turner, Richard F. (66), from England, died September 15, seven miles past North Bluff Fork

Wall, Frederick (31 or 34), and wife, birthplace England

Wall, Sarah Mariah Williamson (or Maria Wheeler) (30), wife, birthplace England

Wall, Joseph (17), and sister, birthplace England. Name also listed in *Journal History*, 11/9/1856, with the words "and wife"

Wall, Emily E. (16), sister, birthplace England

Walter (or Walters or Waters), John (64), birthplace England, died October 25 past Rock Creek

Wandelin (or Vandelin or Vendin or Wendin or Wenden), Lars Gudman (or Gudmanson or Gudmann) (60), from Denmark, died October 24 and was buried at Rock Creek

Ward, Lucy (23), married James Cole on November 2, west of Fort Bridger

Watson, Andrew (24)

West, Sarah (23 or 24), birthplace England

Wheeler, Edward (51 or 52), and family, birthplace England

Wheeler, Ann (54 or 55), wife, birthplace England

Wheeler, Mary (24), birthplace England

Whitham (or Witsom or Withom), Eliza (42), and son

Whitham, Joseph (9), son

Wickland (or Wicklund), Oleo (or Olof or Ole) Jacobsen (30), and family, birthplace Sweden

Wickland, Ella Jonsson (30), wife, birthplace Sweden

Wickland (or Wicklund), Christine (or Christina) (8 or 9), birthplace Sweden

Wickland, Jonas (5 or 6), birthplace Sweden

Wickland (or Wicklund), Sarah Jacobine (or Jacobina) (3), birthplace Denmark

Wickland, Ephramine (or Ephraimuer) Josephine (1), birthplace Denmark

Wickland, Jacob, born October 16 on the Sweetwater

Wilford, William, with Independent Wagons, joined Hodgett company at Fort Laramie

Wilkey (or Wilkie), Isabella (47 or 48),

(had charge of Elizabeth Forbes, 8),
birthplace Scotland
Williams, Mary (50), from England, died
July 23, from eating green plums
Williams, Sarah A. (22), birthplace
England
Willie, James G. (41), Captain, birthplace
England
Witts (or Wit or Witt or Wilts), Samuel H.
(65 or 67), birthplace England, died
October 26 past Rock Creek
Woodward, William (23), birthplace
England

MARTIN HANDCART COMPANY

The following names, ages in May of 1856, and birthplaces have been taken from Leroy R. Hafen and Ann W. Hafen, Handcarts to Zion, 1856–1860 (Glendale, Calif.: The Arthur H. Clark Co., 1960), pp. 295–302; Journal History of The Church of Jesus Christ of Latter-day Saints (Archives, LDS Church Historical Department, Salt Lake City, Utah), 11/9/1856; and Susan Easton Black, Membership of The Church of Jesus Christ of Latter-day Saints, 1830–1848 (Provo, Utah: Brigham Young University Religious Studies Center, 1989), pp. 42–99. Discrepancies and names from other sources are also listed. In this and all other lists, birth and death dates are in 1856 unless specified otherwise.

From Florence, Nebraska, to Salt Lake City, Utah, and those who died previously:

Acres, Joseph (24), and wife, died September 22

Acres, Ann Pugh (23), wife

Allcock, Sarah (66), birthplace England, died May 31 of flux and was buried at sea

Allen, Ann (73), birthplace England, died June 27

Allen, Eliza, and daughter

Allen, Eleanora (or Eleanor) (18), birthplace Ireland

Allen, Elizabeth (43)

Allen, Maria (24)

Allen, James (20)

Allen, George (15)

Allen, Sarah (12)

Allen, Mary (43), birthplace England, died October 6, thirty miles east of Fort Laramie

Allen, Maria (21), daughter of Mary Allen

Anderson, Ann (47), birthplace England

Andrews, John J. (44)

Anglesea (or Anglesey), Martha (22), birthplace England

Ashton, William (33 or 34), father, birthplace England

Ashton, Sarah Ann Barlow (33), mother, birthplace England, died August 26

Ashton, Betsy (11), birthplace England, died en route

Ashton, Sarah (7), birthplace England

Ashton, Mary (4), birthplace England

Ashton, Elizabeth (1 year 5 months or 2), birthplace England, died July 2 in Boston

Ashton, Sarah Ann, daughter, born August 4 on plains of Nebraska, died September 11

Atherton, Ellen (or Hellen) Daniels (57), birthplace England

Bailey, John (49), and family, birthplace England, died in December after arriving in Salt Lake

Bailey, Jane (45), wife, birthplace England

Bailey, Langley (18), birthplace England

Bailey, John (15), birthplace England

Bailey, Thomas (11 or 12), birthplace England

Bailey, David (5), birthplace England

Baker, George (27), birthplace England, died June 1 and was buried at sea

Barlow, Ann (50 or 58), mother, birthplace England

Barlow, John (or Joseph) (17), birthplace England

Barlow, Jane (14 or 15), birthplace England

Barlow, Joseph (7), birthplace England

Barnes, George (41), with wife and children, birthplace England, died on plains

Barnes, Jane Howard (38 or 41), wife, birthplace England

Barnes, Margaret (15), birthplace England

Barnes, Betsy (or Elizabeth) (12), birthplace England

Barnes, Esther (10), birthplace England

Barnes, Deborah (8), birthplace England

Barnes, William L. (5), birthplace England

Barnes, Mary Jane, born July 24 at Council Bluffs, Iowa

Bartholme, Bone (26), birthplace Italy

Barton, William (47), and family, birthplace England, died September 30

Barton, Mary Ann (33 or 36), wife, birthplace England

Barton, Mary (14)

Barton, Francis (3 1/2), birthplace England

Barton, Elizabeth (1 1/2), died July 6

Batchelder (or Batchelor or Bacholer), Emma (20), birthplace England, started in Willie company, then joined Martin company at Fort Laramie

Bedwell, John

Bedwell, Sarah, wife

Beer, Benjamin J. (43 or 44), and wife, birthplace England

Beer, Margaret (or Mary Ann Livesey) (44)

Bennett, Harriet (51 or 53), birthplace England

Beswick, Ann (65)

Beswick, Joseph (33), son

Billingham (or Douglas), Eliza (18), died en route

Binder, William L. S. (23 or 24), husband, birthplace England

Binder, Eliza (24), wife, birthplace England

Bird, Thomas P. (18), birthplace England, died en route

Bitten (or Bitton), John E. (26), and family, birthplace England

Bitten, Jane (19), sister, birthplace England

Bitten, Sarah S. (17), birthplace England

Blackham, Martha (47 or 49), and family, birthplace England

Blackham, Samuel (21), son, birthplace England

Blackham, Sarah (15 or 16), daughter, birthplace England

Blackham, Thomas (13 or 14), son, birthplace England

Blair, David (43 or 45), and family, birthplace Scotland, died en route

Blair, Deborah (39), wife, birthplace England

Blair, Deborah L. B. (7 or 8), birthplace England

Blair, Elizabeth (5), birthplace England

Blair, David (6 months), birthplace England, died en route

Blakey, Richard (36), and family, died en route

Blakey, Caroline Garston (36), wife, birthplace England

Blakey, Caroline, Jr. (16)

Blakey, John Moroni (6 or 9), birthplace England

Blakey, Richard, Jr. (8 months or 2), birthplace England

Bleak, James Godson (26), and family, birthplace England

Bleak, Elizabeth (27 or 28), wife, birthplace England

Bleak, Richard (6), birthplace England

Bleak, Thomas (4), birthplace England

Bleak, James, Jr. (2), birthplace England

Bleak, Mary (infant)

Bodd, Thomas, died en route

Bowes (or Bowers), Elizabeth (27)

Bradshaw, Elizabeth Simpson Haigh (48), and family

Bradshaw, Robert Hall (11), birthplace England

Bradshaw, Isabella Jane (10), birthplace England

Bradshaw, Richard Paul (6), birthplace England

Brice, Richard (51 or 55), and family, birthplace England

Brice, Hannah (50 or 54), wife, birthplace England, died en route

Brice, John (11 or 12), birthplace England

Brice, Jane (9 or 10), birthplace England

Bridge, Alfred (21 or 24), birthplace England, died en route

Briggs, John (42 or 43), birthplace England, died November 3 on plains

Briggs, Ruth Butterworth (39), birthplace England

Briggs, Eliza (19)

Briggs, Thomas (13), birthplace England, died November 11 on plains

Briggs, James (11)

Briggs, Mary Hannah (7 or 9), birthplace England, died November 29 on plains

Briggs, Sarah Ann (4)

Briggs, Rachael (3)

Briggs, Emma (8 months)

Brooks, Nathan (60 or 61) and family, birthplace England

Brooks, Betty (53), wife, birthplace England

Brooks, Alice (21 or 22), birthplace England, daughter of Samuel Brooks and Sarah Ashley

Brown (or Browne), Elizabeth (35)

Brown, Jane (25)

Burge, Francis E. (31), died en route

Bryner, Hans Ulrick, father

Bryner, Barbara (25), daughter

Burton, Eliza Cusworth (32), and family

Burton, Joseph F. (6), birthplace England

Burton, Martha A. (4), birthplace England

Burton, Elizabeth, died July 5 in Toledo

Carter, Ellen (38), birthplace England, wife of John Carter

Carter, John (10), son, birthplace England

Carter, Luke (45), birthplace England, son of Edward Carter and Elizabeth Troup, died on plains of Nebraska

Chatelain, Peter Louis (31)

Clark, Margaret (or Margareta) (27)

Clegg, Jonathan (40), and family, birthplace England

Clegg, Ellen Walmsley (40), wife, birthplace England

Clegg, William (14), birthplace England

Clegg, Alice (8 or 9), birthplace England, died on plains

Clegg, Henry (3), birthplace England

Clegg, Margaret E. (3 months or 6 months), birthplace England

Clevilis, child, died July 5 and was buried at Toledo

Clifton, Robert (50), and family, birthplace England, died en route

Clifton, Mary Matilda Blanchard (45), wife, birthplace England

Clifton, Rebecca (20), birthplace England

Clifton, Sophia (12), birthplace England

Clifton, Ann (6), birthplace England

Cluff, Moses, returning missionary

Collins, Richard (37), and family, birthplace England

Collins, Emma Lawrence (30), wife, birthplace England

Collins, Louisa (9), birthplace England

Collins, Fred James (6 or 7), birthplace England

Collins, David (4), birthplace England

Collins, George (2), birthplace England

Collins, Samuel (4 months), birthplace England

Cook (or Cooke), Jemima (28)

Crane, Ann (23), birthplace England

Crossley, Mary Jarvis (44 or 45), mother, birthplace England

Crossley, Mary Ann (23), birthplace England

Crossley, Joseph (19), birthplace England, died en route

Crossley, Hannah (15), birthplace England

Crossley, Sarah (12 or 13), birthplace England

Crossley, Ephraim (5), birthplace England

Crossley, William (1), grandson

Davis (or Davies), Edmund (32), birthplace England

Davies, Elizabeth Williams

Dearns, Catherine

Dobson, Alice Pickup (48 or 49), mother, birthplace England

Dobson, Mary Ann (23 or 24), birthplace England

Dobson, Thomas (18 or 19), birthplace England

Dobson, Willard (17), birthplace England

Dodd, Thomas (36), and family, died at Red Buttes near Casper, Wyoming

Dodd, Elizabeth Piercy (36 or 39), wife, birthplace England

Dodd, Alma (10), birthplace England

Dodd, Thomas (8), birthplace England

Dodd, Joseph Smith (5 or 6), birthplace England

Dodd, Elizabeth (2), birthplace England

Dodd, Brigham Young (3 months or 5 months), birthplace England

Douglas, John (39 or 40), and family, birthplace England

Douglas (or Douglass), Mary (35 or 36), wife, birthplace England, died July 18 at Rock Island, Illinois

Douglas, William (14), birthplace England, died en route

Dowlass, John, and family

Durham, Thomas (27 or 28), birthplace England

Durham, Mary Morton (27), wife, birthplace England

Eccles, Thomas (37), and family, birthplace England

Eccles, Alice Hardman (34), wife, birthplace England

Eccles, Mary Ann (11), birthplace England

Eccles, Martha (8), birthplace England

Edmonds, Charles (56), birthplace England, died September 13

Edwards, William (28), birthplace England

Edwards, Harriet (16 or 17), wife, birthplace England

Edwards, William (50 to 55), birthplace England, died en route

Elliot, Eliza (17 or 18)

Evans, Thomas (39), from South Wales

Evans, Ann Johns (39), wife

Evans, Thomas (10), son

Evans, Emma (8), daughter

Evans, Hyrum (6), son

Farmer, Elizabeth, died July 6 at Chicago

Foster, Sarah (25), birthplace England

Franklin, Thomas J. (33), and family, birthplace England

Franklin, Jane (33 or 34), wife, birthplace England

Franklin, Lydia (14), birthplace England

Franks, Sarah (21 or 23), birthplace England

Furner, Robert (30)

Furner, William, Jr. (20)

Gibbons, Jane (25 or 26), birthplace England

Giles, Aaron B. (15)

Gourley, Paul (42 or 43), and family, birthplace Scotland, also had two sons working as teamsters in the Hodgett wagon company

Gourley (or Goarley), Ellison Jup (24), wife

Gourley, Nicholas (or Nichalaus or Nicholus) (11 or 12), daughter of Paul from former marriage, birthplace Scotland

Gourley, Janot (or Jenette or Janet) (8), daughter of Paul from former marriage, birthplace Scotland

Gourley, George (5 or 7), son of Paul from former marriage, birthplace Scotland

Gourley (or Goarlay), Paul (3), son of Paul and Ellison Gourley

Gourley, Margaret Glass (9 months), daughter of Paul and Ellison Gourlay, died August 14 at West Scotie on the Middle Fork of the Coon River

Gourley, Baby, born near Fort Laramie; delivered by Emma Batchelor

Green, Charles (26), and family

Green, Ann (22), wife

Green, George (4 months)

Green, Elizabeth (23)

Greening, Mary Ann (27)

Gregory, Ann (63), died September 18 on the Platte in Nebraska

Gregory, Mary (59)

Griffith (or Griffiths), John (45), and family, birthplace England, died en route

Griffith, Mary Elizabeth (30), wife

Griffith, Margaret A. (16), birthplace England

Griffith, John (11), birthplace England, died on plains

Griffith, Jane E. (8), birthplace England

Griffith, Robert L. (or Herbert R.) (5 or 6), birthplace England, died on plains

Grundy, Sarah (41)

Haigh, Samuel (20), brother, birthplace England

Haigh, Sarah Ann (18 or 19), sister, birthplace England

Halford, John (57)

Halford, Mary (or Sarah) (53), wife

Hall, Charles (21), and family

Hall, Elizabeth (24), wife

Hall, Baby Boy of Charles and Sarah Hall of Stratfordshire, England, born June 29

Hansen, George

Hansen, John

Harper, Mary (64), birthplace England, died en route

Harrison, Samuel

Harrison, William (40 or 41), and family, birthplace England

Harrison, Hannah Ellis (38), wife, birthplace England

Harrison, Aaron (18), birthplace England

Harrison, George (14), birthplace England

Harrison, Mary Ann (12), birthplace England

Harrison, Alice (10), birthplace England

Harrison, Olivia (6), birthplace England

Harrison, Hannah, Jr. (2), birthplace England

Harrison, Sarah Ellen (1 month or 5 months), birthplace England

Hartle (or Hartley), John (70), and family, died en route

Hartle, Lydia (71), wife, died September 17

Hartle, Mary (36), daughter, birthplace England, died September 27

Hartle, William (40)

Hartle, Elizabeth (43)

Hartle, John (12)

Hartle, Samuel (6)

Hartle, William (3)

Hartle, Ephriam (11 months), died October 6, twenty-seven miles west of Scottsbluff

Hartley, Eliza (or Elizabeth) Gill (39), and family

Hartley, Mathilda Jane (21 or 17), birthplace England

Hartley, Sarah (17 or 19), birthplace England

Hartley, Samuel (13)

Hartley, Josephine (10), birthplace England

Hartley, Farewell Harrison (7), birthplace England

Haslam, Esther (50), mother

Haslam, Joseph (18), son

Hawkey, Hannah (33), and family, birthplace England

Hawkey, James (14), birthplace England, died en route

Hawkey, Margaret (4), birthplace England

Hawkey, Hannah, Jr. (3), birthplace England

Haydock (or Haydocke), Elizabeth (45 or 55), mother, birthplace England

Haydock, Mary (21), daughter

Henshall, David (41)

Herring, Mary (35)

Herring, George (16), son

Heycock (or Haycock), Elizabeth (45)

Hicks, Ann (or Annie) (19 or 20), birthplace England

Higgs, Lydia (39 or 45), birthplace England

Hill, Mary (48)

Hill, William (48), father

Hill, William, Jr. (9), son

Hiott, John (33)

Holt, Robert (42), and family, birthplace England

Holt, Ellen Walker (44), wife, birthplace England

Holt, Margaret (23 or 24), birthplace England

Holt, James (21 or 22), birthplace England

Holt, Daniel (15 or 16), birthplace England

Holt, Alice (13), birthplace England

Holt, Joseph (3 or 11), birthplace England

Holt, Martha (5), birthplace England

Hooker (or Hooper), Lydia E. (20), later married S. S. Jones, also a member of the Martin company

Horrocks, Mary (19), sister to Elizabeth Horrocks Jackson and traveling with the Jackson family

Housley, Harriet Agnes Cook (43 or 44), mother, birthplace England

Housley, George (19), son, birthplace England

Howard, William (10)

Hulst (or Hurst), Sarah (49)

Hunter, George (19), died en route

Hunter, James (23)

Hunter, John (18)

Jackson, Aaron (31 or 32), and family, birthplace England, died October 19

Jackson, Elizabeth Horrocks (29), wife, birthplace England

Jackson, Martha Ann (7), birthplace England

Jackson, Mary Elizabeth (4), birthplace England

Jackson, Aaron (2), birthplace England

Jackson, Ann (50)

Jackson, Elizabeth (23)

Jackson, Martha (21)

Jackson, Joseph (16)

Jackson, Samuel (12)

Jackson, Nephi (10)

Jackson, Charles (60), and family, birthplace England, died en route

Jackson, Mary Loxam (62), wife, birthplace England, died en route

Jackson, William (21 or 22), birthplace England

Jackson, Robert, brother

Jackson, William, brother, traveling with their sister, Maria Jackson Normanton, and her family

Jackson, James (47)

Jackson, Samuel (39), and family, husband

Jackson, June (or Jane) (75), Samuel's mother, died October 5

Jackson, Alice (41), wife

Jackson, Lydia C. (15), daughter

Jaques, Ann (42)

Jaques, Caroline (16), daughter

Jaques (or Jacques), John (29), and family, birthplace England

Jaques, Zilpah Loader (24), wife, birthplace England

Jaques, Flora Loader (1), birthplace England, died November 22 or 23

Jaques, Alpha Loader, born August 27 at Cutler's Park, Nebraska

Jarvis, Sam, with family; his wife is listed as head of family on several lists

Jervis (or Jarvis), Amelia, wife

Johnson (or Johnston), Ann (18 or 32)

Johnson (or Johnston), Elizabeth (50), birthplace England

Jones, William (73), and family, died en route; his wife is listed as head of family on several lists

Jones, Sarah Bradshaw (55), wife, birthplace England

Jones, Samuel S. (19), birthplace England

Jones, Albert (16), birthplace England

Jones, William Mason (24), birthplace England, died September 27

Jupp, Mary (35 or 36), birthplace England

Keetch, William (45)

Kemer, Richard

Kewley, James (53 or 54), and family, birthplace England

Kewley, Ann Karran (45 or 41 or 54), wife, birthplace England

Kewley, Margaret (16), birthplace England

Kewley, Robert (11), birthplace England

Kewley, Thomas (3), birthplace England, died July 4 at Cleveland, Ohio

Kimp (Kemp), Henry (25)

Kirkman, Robert Lomax (34), and family, birthplace England, died on plains

Kirkman, Mary Lawson (33), wife

Kirkman, Robert (10), birthplace England

Kirkman, John (8), birthplace England

Kirkman, Joseph (6), birthplace England

Kirkman, Hiram (4), birthplace England

Kirkman, James (2), birthplace England

Kirkman, Peter, born July 9 in Iowa City, Iowa, died on plains

Larsen (or Johansen), Mary Kjirstine (6)

Lattman, Hans Heinrick (50)

Lattman, Elizabeth F., wife

Lattman, Barbara

Lattman, Elizabeth

Lattman, Pauline

Lattman, Gerold

Laurey, Brother, died en route

Lawley, George (55), birthplace England, died October 6

Leah, James (55 or 58), husband, birthplace England, died en route

Leah, Sarah M. Berry (59), wife, birthplace England, died October 4

Ledden, Richard, and family

Ledden, Elizabeth (16)

Ledden, Esther (14)

Leishman, John

Leishman, Jean A., wife

Leishman, Robert (17)

Leishman, John

Lister, John Henry (16)

Lloyd, Ann (36)

Lloyd, Jane (7)

Lloyd (or Loynd), James, Sr. (41 or 50), and family

Lloyd, Elizabeth T. (46), wife

Lloyd, John (19)

Lloyd, James (18)

Lloyd, Thomas (16)

Lloyd, Joseph (13)

Lloyd, Richard (10)

Lloyd, John

Loader, James (56), and family, birthplace England, died September 25 or 27 on plains

Loader, Amy Britwell (54), wife

Loader, Patience (29)

Loader, Tamar (22), daughter, birthplace England

Loader, Maria (19)

Loader, Jane (15)

Loader, Sarah (12)

Loader, Robert (10), died on plains

Lord, Charles (39), and family, birthplace England

Lord, Mary Hentwistle (36), birthplace England

Lubbock, James, and family (listed under Stimpson, William)

Lubbock, Susan H., wife, died en route

Marchant, Caroline (25)

Marshall, Mariann (34), and daughter

Marshall, Emily (9)

Martin, Edward, Captain (37 or 38), birthplace England

Martin, Eliza (20)

Massey (or Maisey), Daniel (38), and family

Massey, Rebecca (34), wife

Massey, Silas (6)

Massey, George (4)

Massey, Rebecca (1 1/2)

Mathis, John

Mattison (or Mattinson), Robert (52), and family, birthplace England, died October 15

Mattison, Ann Shaw (44), wife

Mattison, Robert Jr. (20), birthplace England

Mattison, John (15 or 16), birthplace England

Mattison, George (12), birthplace England

Mattison, Elizabeth Ann (3), birthplace England

Mayne (or Maine), John (24), died October 5

Mayo (or Mayoh), Peter (40 or 50), and family, birthplace England

Mayo, Ann Howarth (40 or 41), wife, birthplace England

Mayo, Mary Elizabeth (8 or 9), birthplace England

Mayo, Noah (1 or 6), birthplace England

McBride, Robert (52), and family, birthplace Scotland, died October 20

McBride, Margaret Howard (41), wife

McBride, Jeanetta Ann (16), birthplace England

McBride, Heber Robert (12 or 13), birthplace England

McBride, Ether Enos (8 or 9), birthplace Scotland

McBride, Peter Howard (6), birthplace Scotland

McBride, Margaret Alice (2 or 3), birthplace England

Mee, Charlotte (22)

Mee, Betsy (14)

Meldrum, George, from Scotland

Meldrum, Jane B. Barclay, wife

Meldrum, James Lowe (2), from Scotland

Mellor, James (37), and family, birthplace England

Mellor, Mary Ann Payne (36 or 37), wife, birthplace England

Mellor, Louisa (15), birthplace England

Mellor, Charlotte Elizabeth (14 or 15), birthplace England

Mellor, Mary Ann (10), birthplace England

Mellor, James, Jr. (7 or 8), birthplace England

Mellor, William Charles (5), birthplace England

Mellor, Emma Marintha (2), twin, birthplace England

Mellor, Clara Althera (2), twin, birthplace England

Mellor, Eliza, twin, born and died in May 1856, in Liverpool, England, as company boarded ship

Mellor, Elizabeth, twin, born and died in May 1856, in Liverpool, England, as company boarded ship

Middleton, William (39 or 40), and family, birthplace England

Middleton, Amy Parsons (or Parson) (43 or 48), wife

Middleton, John (15)

Mignell, Sarah, and family

Mitchell, Mary (35), and son

Mitchell, James (4)

Moon, Child, died July 4 and was buried at Buffalo, New York

Moore (or Moores), Elizabeth (26)

Mores (or Moores), Sarah Jane (2), died July 3, at Buffalo, New York

Morley, Sarah A. Wood (29), birthplace England

Morton, Joshua

Morton, Harriet Schofield, wife

Morton, Eliza (20), daughter

Moss, Joseph (49), and family, birthplace England

Moss, Mary Brabin (44 or 45), wife, birthplace England

Moss, Edward (20 or 21), birthplace England

Moss, Peter John (18), birthplace England

Moss, Joseph, Jr. (15), birthplace England

Moss, James (12), birthplace England

Moss, Alice (10), birthplace England

Moss, Hiram (or Hyram) Ralph (7 or 8), birthplace England

Munn, Edward Fredrick (22), birthplace England

Murdock (or Murdoch), Mary (72 or 73), birthplace Scotland, died October 3

Nightingale, Jane Archer (57), and family, birthplace England

Nightingale, Sarah Ann (29 or 31), birthplace England

Nightingale, Jemima (21), birthplace England

Nightingale, Joseph (16), birthplace England

Normandson, Thomas (38), died en route

Normington, Thomas (37 or 38), and family, birthplace England, died in November

Normington, Maria (or Mariah or Marie) Jackson (36), wife, birthplace England

Normington, Lavinia (10), birthplace England

Normington, Mary Ellen (8), birthplace England

Normington, Hannah (6), birthplace England

Normington, Robert R. (or Euphraim Robert) (4), birthplace England, died

Normington, Daniel (1), birthplace England, died August 12

Oldham, John (33), and family, birthplace England

Oldham, Sarah Hodgkison (23), wife, birthplace England

Oldham, Jane Eliza (or Jane Elizabeth) (4), birthplace England

Oldham, Louis William (6 months), birthplace England

Ollerton (or Oleston), John (55 or 56), and family, birthplace England, died November 30

Ollerton, Alice Dandy (53), wife, birthplace England, died November 30

Ollerton, Alice (19), birthplace England, died December 30

Ollerton, Jane Ann (15), birthplace England

Ollerton, Sarah (6), birthplace England

Openshaw, William, Jr. (60 or 50), and family, birthplace England

Openshaw, Ann Walmsley Greenhalgh (50), wife, birthplace England

Openshaw, Samuel (22), birthplace England

Openshaw, Eli (or Eliza Booth) (21), birthplace England, died en route

Openshaw, Levi (19), birthplace England

Openshaw, Mary C. (15 or 17), birthplace England

Openshaw, Eleanor (14), birthplace England

Openshaw, Mary Ann (10), birthplace England

Ord, Thomas (29), husband, birthplace England

Ord, Eleanor Grant (26), wife, birthplace England

Orme, Amy Kirby (52 or 53), and family, birthplace England

Orme, Sarah Ann (32 or 29), birthplace England

Orme, Samuel Washington (23 or 24), birthplace England

Orme, Rebecca (18 or 21), birthplace England

Padley, George W. (20), birthplace England, was engaged to Sarah Franks and died at Martin's Cove

Palmer, Richard (9 1/2), died July 1, of measles, in Boston

Parker, Caroline (36), spinster

Parker, Esther (37), and family

Parker, Ellen (8)

Parker, Priscilla (5)

Parkinson, John (37 or 38), and family, birthplace England, died on plains

Parkinson, Ellen Smalley (37), birthplace England, died on plains

Parkinson, Samuel (17 or 18), birthplace England, turned back

Parkinson, Joseph (15 or 16), birthplace England, died on plains

Parkinson, Elizabeth Jane (10 or 11), birthplace England

Parkinson, Margaret (8 or 9), birthplace England

Parkinson, John (7), birthplace England

Parkinson, Ellen (5), birthplace England

Parkinson, Mary (3), birthplace England, died July 25 on plains

Parkinson, Esther (or Ether) (2), birthplace England, died on plains

Parkinson, William (infant), birthplace England, died July 20 on plains

Parks, Elizabeth H. (26)

Parks, Esther, and family

Patching, Susannah (47)

Paxman, William Horizon, son of William and Ann Paxman, born June 12 on ship Horizon

Pearce (or Pierce), Robert (31)

Pears, Eliza (19), mother, birthplace England

Pears, Baby Girl, daughter, born and died May 31, buried at sea

Pears, John (57), and family, died on plains

Pears, Anna W., wife

Pears, Margaret

Pears, Eliza (14)

Pears, Rose (54)

Peel, John (41 or 58), and family, birthplace England, died November 12

Peel, Anna (or Hannah) Rhoades (41), wife, birthplace England

Peel, Naomi Annie (8), birthplace England

Peel, Marintha Althera (5), birthplace England

Peyton, Nathaniel (58), and family

Peyton, Margaret (37), wife

Peyton, Eliza (12 weeks)

Platt (or Pratt), Benjamin (23), husband, birthplace England

Platt, Mary Graves (19), wife

Porrit, Thomas, and family

Porrit (or Parrit or Porritt), Margaret McCann (40), wife, birthplace England, shown as head of family on several lists

Porrit, Nathaniel (15), birthplace England

Porrit, Rebecca (12 or 13), birthplace England

Porrit, Thomas (6 or 7), birthplace England

Pucell (or Purcell), Samuel (50 or 51), and family, birthplace England, died October 22

Pucell, Margaret Perren (53), wife, birthplace England, died October 27

Pucell, Ann (24 or 25), birthplace England

Pucell, Margaret Agusta, Jr. (14), birthplace England

Pucell, Ellen (9 or 10), birthplace England

Pucell (or Purcell), William (25), son of Samuel and Margaret above, and family, birthplace England

Pucell, Eliza Schofield (24 or 25), wife, birthplace England

Pucell, Robert (3 months), birthplace England

Purcell, Elizabeth

Purcell, Robert

Purson, John

Quin (or Quinn), Mary Ann Hosking (49), and family, birthplace England

Quin, William R. (24), birthplace British Isles

Quin, Mary Ann, Jr. (22), birthplace British Isles

Quin, Harriet (18 or 19), birthplace British Isles

Quin, Elizabeth (16 or 17), birthplace British Isles

Quin, George (13 or 14), birthplace British Isles

Quin, Isabella (7 or 8), birthplace British Isles

Quin, Joseph Hyrum (5), birthplace British Isles

Ramsden, Samuel (45), and family, birthplace England

Ramsden, Esther (43), wife, birthplace England

Ramsden, Samuel C. (12), birthplace England

Rhead (or Reed or Read), Samuel George (48 or 49), and family, birthplace England

Rhead, Elizabeth Georgina Quilley (50), wife, birthplace England

Rhead, Elitha (or Alicia) Quilley (15), birthplace England

Rhead, Samuel Milford (14), birthplace England

Rhead, Frisbea (or Thisbe or Thisbea) Quilley (9 or 11), birthplace England

Rhead, Walter Pyramus (6 or 7), birthplace England

Riley, Mary Ann Malley (39), and son, birthplace England

Riley, Thomas Katen (11 or 12), birthplace England

Robinson, Frederic C. (29), husband, birthplace England

Robinson, Elizabeth Gambles (17), wife, birthplace England

Robinson, Solomon (23), brother, birthplace England, died November 5

Robinson, Elizabeth (19), sister, birthplace England

Robison (or Robinson), Margaret (52), and family

Robinson, Dorothy (32)

Robinson, Elizabeth (17)

Robinson, George (12)

Rodwell, John (55), and wife, birthplace England

Rodwell, Sarah (59), wife, birthplace England

Rogerson, Mary Harrison Ferron (52 or 54), and family, birthplace England

Rogerson, James (25 or 26), birthplace England

Rogerson, Bridget (23 or 24), birthplace England

Rogerson, William (22), birthplace England

Rogerson, Josiah (15), birthplace England

Rogerson, Sarah Ann (12 or 13), birthplace England

Rogerson, John Edward (9), birthplace England

Ryle (or Royle), Sarah Moss (64 or 67), birthplace England

Scott, Mary (63), birthplace England, died August 18 near camp at Wishmabotna on the Turkey River

Sculthorpe, George John (47)

Seddon, Richard (36)

Seddon, Elizabeth (16)

Seddon, Esther (12)

Sermon, Joseph (53), died on plains

Sermon, Elizabeth Whitear (37), wife

Sermon, John (9)

Sermon, Henry (7)

Sermon, Robert (5)

Sermon, Marian (or Mary Ann) (3)

Severn, William Thomas (19), and wife, birthplace England

Severn, Mary Astle (19), birthplace

England, married on ship *Horizon* on May 29

Shorten, John Bussey (20), birthplace England, stayed at Devil's Gate

Shorter (or Shorton), James (14)

Sorenson, Jeppe

Sorenson, Anna Catherine, wife (20)

Southwell, John William (20 or 23)

Speakman, Hannah (18 or 19), birthplace England

Squires, Henry Agustus (or Augustus) (30 or 31), and family, birthplace England

Squires, Sarah Minnie Cattlin (or Catlin) (28 or 29), wife, birthplace England

Squires, Sarah Augusta (8), birthplace England

Squires, Mary Emily (5 or 6), birthplace England

Squires, Catherine Harriet (4 or 5), birthplace England

Squires, Clara Annie (3), birthplace England

Squires, Rosetta Agnes (11 months or 1), birthplace England

Squires, Echo, born November 26 in Echo Canyon, Utah

Steele (or Steel), James (29), and family, birthplace Scotland, died November 10 near Bitter Creek

Steele, Elizabeth Wylie (28 or 29), wife, birthplace Scotland

Steele, James Ephraim (3), birthplace England

Steele, William George (1), birthplace England

Stimpson, William (33), and family

Stimpson, Rebecca Lubbock (31), wife, also daughter of James and Susan Lubbock, died en route

Stimpson, Frederick (4)

Stimpson, William (18 months or 2 years), son, died September 26

Stinson, Samuel, and family

Stone, Jonathan (or John W.) (53), died October 19 at Last Crossing of the Platte at Casper

Stone, Granddaughter, died at Last Crossing of the Platte at Casper

Stones, James (32), and family, birthplace England

Stones, Mary Millnes (or Milnes) (34), wife, birthplace England

Stones, Hannah Rachel (7 or 10), birthplace England

Stones, Sarah Elizabeth (7), birthplace England

Stones, John O. (or John Charles) (4 or 5), birthplace England

Stones, Erastus J. (or James Erastus or James D.) (3), birthplace England

Tann, Catherine (16)

Tasker, Andrew (52), birthplace England

Taylor, Elizabeth (53), and family, birthplace England; her daughter Sarah was in the Hodgett company

Taylor, James (39), birthplace England, died en route

Taylor, Elizabeth (18)

Taylor, Joseph (44), died October 8, one mile before Fort Laramie, during the first snow; his daughter and her husband, William and Mary Upton, were also in the company

Taylor, Harriet Sidwell (49), wife, died November 10 near Martin's Cove

Taylor, Joseph

Taylor, Elizabeth (or Eliza) (44), wife

Taylor, Mary Soar (31), and family, birthplace England

Taylor, William Henry (12), birthplace England

Taylor, Jesse Soar (9 or 10), birthplace England

Thirkman, Robert

Thomas, Ann Jane (14), birthplace Wales

Thomas, James

Thompson, John (30), and family, birthplace England

Thompson, Mary (29), wife, birthplace England

Thompson, Mary Jane (9), birthplace England

Thompson (or Thomson), Moses (24), birthplace Scotland, died on the Sweetwater near Devil's Gate

Thorn (or Thorne), James (56)

Thornton, Hannah (29), and family, birthplace England

Thornton, Wardeman (8 or 9), birthplace England

Thornton, Amanda (5), birthplace England

Thornton, Sarah Ann (3), birthplace England

Till, Robert

Till, Sister, wife

Toone, John (43), birthplace England

Turner, Robert (30)

Turner, William

Twelves, Charles (37), and family, birthplace England

Twelves, Ann Elizabeth Henrietta Gunn (36), wife, birthplace England

Twelves, Charles Samuel (13), birthplace England, died in November

Twelves, John Robert (11), birthplace England

Twelves, Ann Elizabeth Henrietta (7), birthplace England

Twelves, Orson (4 or 6), birthplace England

Twelves, Brigham (2 or 3), birthplace England, died August 11

Twelves, Mary Jane, born June 27

Tyler, Daniel, made aide to Captain Martin at Florence

Upton, William (22), husband, birthplace England, died and was buried with his mother-in-law, Harriet Taylor, probably at Martin's Cove

Upton, Mary Taylor (20), wife, daughter of Joseph and Harriet Taylor; later married her rescuer, William Bert Simmons

Upton, Baby. One source indicates that Mary "lost a baby along the way"

Venner, Richard (70), died September 30

Walker, William T. (43)

Walker, James (28). One reference indicates he was married to Sarah; another shows him married to a Barbara

Walker, Sarah R. (or Sarah Ann or Barbara) (24)

Walsh, William (29 or 30), and family, birthplace England, died in November on plains

Walsh, Alice Fish (27 or 29 or 25), wife, birthplace England

Walsh, Robert (4), birthplace England, died September 13

Walsh, John (3), birthplace England

Walsh, Sarah (5 months), birthplace England

Walworth (or Wallwork), Thomas (27)

Walworth, William (6), son

Ward, William

Ward, Jane Rogers, wife

Ward, David

Wardell (or Wardle), Hannah (35)

Wardle, Isaac John (20), birthplace England

Watkins, John (22), and family, birthplace England

Watkins, Margaret Ackhurst (23 or 24), wife, birthplace England

Watkins, Elizabeth (4), birthplace England

Watkins, John T. (1 1/2), birthplace England

Watts, Charles O. (18)

Waugh, George P. (68), birthplace England, died en route

Webster, Francis (25 or 26), and family, birthplace England

Webster, Ann Elizabeth (or Elizabeth Ann) Parsons (or Parson) (24), wife, birthplace England

Webster, Amy Elizabeth, born September 27 in Nebraska

White, Elias (25), and family

White, Elizabeth (23)

White, George Washington

White, Alice Ellenor (infant)

White, Eliza (18)

White, Maria (55), birthplace England

Whittaker, Robert (64)

Whittaker, William, died October 30 and was buried at Willow Springs, Wyoming

Whittaker, Robert (19), birthplace England

Wignall, Sarah (48), and family, birthplace England

Wignall, Mary Ann (25 or 16), birthplace England

Wignall, Sarah J. (16 or 25), birthplace England

Wignall (or Wignol), William (33), and family, birthplace England

Wignall, Grace Slater (33 or 35), wife, birthplace England

Wignall, Joseph Smith (11), birthplace England

Wignall, Mary (8 or 9), birthplace England

Wignall, James (7), birthplace England

Wignall, Jane (4 or 5), birthplace England

Wignall, Grace (2 or 3), birthplace England

Wignall, William H. (3 months), birthplace England

Wiley (or Wylie), Mary (66)

Wilkinson, Charles (40), husband, birthplace England, drove wagon and family

Wilkinson, Sarah Hughes (40), wife, birthplace England, only Wilkinson on Hafen list

Wilkinson, Joseph Thomas, son (9)

Wilkinson, Sarah Jane (6), daughter, died in Iowa City

Wilkinson, Mary (4), daughter, died in Iowa City

Williamson, Ann Roper (48 or 52), and family, birthplace England

Williamson, Ellen (23), birthplace England

Williamson, Ann (16 or 19), birthplace England

Williamson, Mary (16)

Williamson, William (13)

Williamson, John (11)

Williamson, Betsy (3)

Williamson, Sarah (20)

Wilson, James (25 or 26), and family, birthplace England

Wilson, Elizabeth Oilerton (or Ollerton) (24), wife

Wilson, Nancy Horizon, born May 27 on ship *Horizon,* died June 19 and was buried at sea

Wilson, Sister, captured by Indians, presumed dead

Wilson, Baby, killed by Indians August 25, nine miles west of Prairie Creek, Nebraska

Winn (or Wynn), Jane Broughton, mother, died in Wyoming

Winn, Mary Anne (11), daughter

Wood, John B.

Woodcock, Charles (52), birthplace England, died September 20 on plains

Woodcock, Joseph (29), husband, birthplace England

Woodcock, Jane (34 or 37), birthplace England

Woodcock, John (20)

Woodhead, John (19 or 20), birthplace England

Woods, Peter (75), died en route

Woods, Mary (59)

Wright, Elizabeth Adamson (58 or 59), and daughter, birthplace England

Wright, Elizabeth (22 or 32), birthplace England

Wright, Rachel Watts (46), mother, birthplace England

Wright, Charles (13), birthplace England

Wright, John (42), birthplace England, died August 12, of ague and fever, buried at South Skunk River

Wright, Thomas

Wright, Sarah Ann Britt (29)

Wright, James B. (11)

Wright, Thomas (4)

Wright, Emma Mariah (1 1/2), daughter

Wrigley (or Rigley), Ann (60)

Yam, Catherine

HUNT WAGON COMPANY

The following names, ages, and birthplaces have been taken from Journal History of The Church of Jesus Christ of Latter-day Saints (Archives, LDS Church Historical Department, Salt Lake City, Utah), reports of the Hunt wagon company on October 15, 1856, pp. 2–3 and December 15, 1856, pp. 2–37. Discrepancies and names from other sources are also listed.

From Iowa City, Iowa, to Salt Lake City, Utah:

Allen, George R. (24), birthplace England, butcher

Ashbrook, Ann (25), birthplace England

Austin, George (20), birthplace England, laborer

Autchinson, Mary, birthplace England

Barman, James, returned to Laramie on October 12 because of weak team

Barman, May (or Mary), died at Devil's Gate

Barton, William (26), birthplace England, laborer

Baxter, Henry (50), birthplace Scotland, miner

Baxter, Agnes (50), birthplace Scotland

Baxter, Magdalen (or Magdalene) (24), birthplace Scotland

Baxter, Jane (18), birthplace Scotland

Baxter, Agnes (15), birthplace Scotland

Beasley (or Beesley), William (48), husband, birthplace England, bootmaker. Family returned October 12 to Fort Laramie

Beasley, Ann (48), birthplace England

Beasley, Mary A. (17), birthplace England

Beasley, Sarah F. (11), birthplace England

Bell, William (41 or 44), husband, birthplace England, biscuit baker. Family returned October 12 to Fort Laramie

Bell, Sarah (50), wife, birthplace England

Bell, Sarah (8), daughter, birthplace England

Bills, Brother, husband

Bills, Sister, wife

Boderick (or Broderick), Thomas B. (31), husband, birthplace England, brickmaker

Boderick, Elizabeth (22), birthplace England

Bowen, David (33), birthplace Wales

Bowen, Jane Foster (35 or 33), wife, birthplace Wales

Bowen, William Perry (11), son, birthplace Wales

Bowen, George Foster (7), son, birthplace Wales

Bowen, Eleanor Jane (or Ellen Jane) (4), daughter, birthplace Wales

Bowen, John Evans (1), son, birthplace Wales

Braby, George (23), birthplace England, baker

Braby, Sarah (24), birthplace England

Brenchley (or Birchley), Caroline (24), birthplace England

Briner (or Bryner), Olrich (or Ulrich) (29 or 24), husband, birthplace Switzerland, butcher

Briner, Maria A. (28), wife, birthplace Switzerland

Briner, Maria (5), child, birthplace Switzerland

Briner, Susannah (66), mother to Olrich Briner, birthplace Switzerland, died en route

Brooks, Edmund J. (24), birthplace England, seaman

Brooks, Eliza White (28), birthplace England

Brooks, Thomas, husband

Brooks, Elizabeth Harper, wife, birthplace England

Brooks, George Finly (22), son, birthplace England, seaman

Brown, Hester (or Esther) (22), birthplace Isle of Man, milliner

Bruner, Susannah (64), birthplace Switzerland, died October 4, five miles before Chimney Rock

Burlington (or Bellington), Ruth (64), birthplace England

Burton, William (26), died November 6, of ague and cold, at Devil's Gate

Busley, William

Chapple (or Chaple), John, stayed at Devil's Gate

Chapple, Elijah, birthplace England, painter and glazier

Clark, Rebecca (22), birthplace England

Cotton, Elizabeth (15), birthplace England

Creek, James (34), birthplace England, lawyer, Captain of 10 and assistant to the Captain of the Guard

Cunison, John

Cutcliff (or Cutcliffe), Mary J. (22), birthplace England

Dalrymple, Henry H., Captain of 10

Davis, Elias (44), birthplace England, laborer; died September 21 on the Platte River, fifty-eight miles past Fort Kearny

Davis, Ann (47), wife, birthplace England, died November 7 at Devil's Gate

Davis (or David), David (36), birthplace Wales, collier

Davis, Elizabeth (42), birthplace Wales

Davis, Sarah (33), birthplace Wales

Davis, Nathan, Captain of 10

Dee, John (56), husband, birthplace Wales, crutemaker

Dee, Margaret (56), wife, birthplace Wales

Dee, Thomas (25), son, birthplace Wales

Dee, Ann (21), daughter, birthplace Wales

Dee, Hannah (12), daughter, birthplace Wales

Dee, John (8), son, birthplace Wales

Dee, Dan C. (3 months), born on ship *Samuel Curling*

Derry, George (30), husband, birthplace England, harnessmaker

Derry, Louisa (31), wife, birthplace England

Derry, Charles H. (6), son, birthplace England

Derry, Moroni (3), son, birthplace England

Derry, Joseph (34), birthplace England

Dow, Alexander (56), birthplace Scotland, coppersmith

Dow, John (3), birthplace Scotland

Ellis, John (38), birthplace Wales, carpenter, stayed at Devil's Gate

Ennion, John (50), birthplace England, gardener

Ennion, Mary E. (50), wife, birthplace England

Evans, Hannah (35), birthplace Wales

Evans, Samuel (36), birthplace Wales, collier

Evans, Sarah (46), birthplace Wales

Farmer, James (39), husband, birthplace England, mason

Farmer, Mary Ann Biddie (26), wife, birthplace England

Farmer, Emma J. (12), daughter, birthplace England

Farmer, Agnes A. (10), daughter, birthplace England

Farmer, Elizabeth (8), daughter, birthplace England

Farmer, Mary Ann (28), birthplace England

Fredrickson, Hans P. (or Lars Peter) (15), birthplace Denmark

Galbraithe, John (27), birthplace Scotland, engine driver, stayed at Devil's Gate

Gardner, William (26), birthplace England

Gaskell, Elizabeth (40), birthplace England

Gilbert, Brother

Giles, Joseph (7)

Giles, Hyrum (6)

Goble, William (39), husband, birthplace England, gardener

Goble, Mary (43), wife, birthplace England, died December 11 between Little and Big Mountains

Goble, Mary (13), daughter, birthplace England

Goble, Edwin (10), son, birthplace England

Goble, Caroline (8), daughter, birthplace England

Goble, Harriet (6), daughter, birthplace England

Goble, James (4), son, birthplace England, died at Devil's Gate

Goble, Fanny (2), daughter, birthplace England, died July 19, of measles, at Iowa City

Goble, Edith (infant), daughter, born September 23, died November 3 on Platte River

Goodey, Lousee (30), birthplace England

Grant, Susan (56), Scotland

Grant, Thomas (18), birthplace Scotland

Grant, Elizabeth (13), birthplace Scotland

Griffiths, Richard (40), birthplace Wales, collier

Hancock, William (21), birthplace England, painter and glazier

Handy, William (39), birthplace England, laborer, stayed at Devil's Gate

Hardcastle, Ann Hall (46), and family

Hardcastle, Mary Ann (22)

Hardcastle, John D. (18), birthplace England, engine driver, stayed at Devil's Gate

Hardcastle, Elizabeth (16)

Hardcastle, Levi

Hardcastle, Joseph

Hardcastle, Emma (8)

Haven, Jessie (42), missionary

Haycock, Elizabeth (44), birthplace England

Haycock, William, birthplace England

Henning, Jane (21), birthplace England, confectioner

Hicks, John (31), birthplace England, shoemaker

Hicks, Harriet (26), birthplace England

Hill, Mary Ann Smith White (60), birthplace England

Hill, Mary (48)

Holly (or Holley), Charles (35), birthplace England, stonemason, Captain of the Guard

Holly, Mary (26), birthplace England

Holly (or Holley), Henry (28), birthplace England, laborer

Holly, Lucy Meadows (22), birthplace England

Holly (or Holley), James (31), birthplace England, laborer, Captain of 10 after James Creek

Holly, Lucy J. (or Sarah J.) (21), birthplace England

Holly, Ann (3), birthplace England

Holly, James H. (1), birthplace England

Holly, Henry, birthplace England

Hookey, Thomas (61), birthplace England, blacksmith

Hookey, Hannah (47), birthplace England

Hopkins, Mary (7), birthplace Wales

Horten, John B., birthplace England

Hunt, John A. (26), birthplace England, returning missionary from Great Britain, began as Captain of 50 and succeeded Captain Dan Jones as Captain of the entire wagon train

Hutchinson, Mary (70), birthplace England, died November 11, three days after leaving Devil's Gate

Jakeman, Henry (23), birthplace England, printer, stayed at Devil's Gate

James, Ruth (21), birthplace Wales

Jenkens (or Jenkins), Rossar (or Rossiter) (21), collier, stayed at Devil's Gate

Jenkins, Morris (34), birthplace Wales, farmer

Jenkins, Margaret (34), birthplace Wales

Jenkins, Eliza (14), birthplace Wales

Jenkins, John (10), birthplace Wales

Jenkins, Thomas (4), birthplace Wales

Jenkins, Moses, Captain of 10

Johnson, Ann (18), birthplace England

Jones, Dan, Captain of 100, was in charge of both the Hunt and Hodgett Companies from July 13 to August 11. He then was released and Captain Hunt was put in charge

Jones, Ellis

Jones, Joel

Jones, John (40), birthplace Wales, coal proprietor

Jones, Elias (46), birthplace Wales, coal proprietor

Jones, Hannah (38), birthplace Wales

Jones, Mary (18), birthplace Wales

Jones, John (14), birthplace Wales

Jones, Llewellen (or Llewellyn) (12), birthplace Wales

Jones, Anne (or Ann) (10), birthplace Wales

Jones, Elias (7), birthplace Wales

Jones, Ruth (5), birthplace Wales

Jones, Thomas (4), birthplace Wales

Jones, Thomas (70), birthplace Wales

Jones, Sister

Jones, Ruth, daughter, born October 6, just past Scottsbluff, Nebraska

Jub (or Jubb), Ann (33), birthplace England

Kingman, Ann (20), birthplace England

Knight, Hannah (27), birthplace England

Latey, William (20), birthplace England, carpenter, stayed at Devil's Gate

Latrille (or Latrielle), Mary Matilda (22), birthplace England

Latrille, Rachel (or Rachael) (55), birthplace England

Leaing (or Leainy), Elizabeth (72), birthplace Scotland

Lewis, John (31), husband, birthplace Wales, ladler, Captain of 10

Lewis, Elizabeth (33), wife, birthplace Wales

Lewis, George H. (7), son, birthplace Wales

Lewis, Elizabeth (3), daughter, birthplace Wales

Lewis, Llewellyn (16), spinner

Lewis, Rufus (26), birthplace Wales, wool spinner

Linforth, James (29)

Linforth, Mary J. (29)

Linforth, Frank O. (3)

Linforth, Edward W. (2)

Linforth, Alfred (18)

Malin, Ann (24), birthplace England, cook for Hunt company

May, George (24), birthplace England, clerk

May, Sister, died somewhere near Devil's Gate

McDonald, George Rust (28), birthplace Scotland

McDonald, Martha R. (35), birthplace Scotland

McDonald, Lemuel I. (1), birthplace Scotland

McMurrin, Joseph (33), husband, birthplace Scotland, cooper

McMurrin, Margaret (32), wife, birthplace Scotland

McMurrin, Margaret (10), daughter, birthplace Scotland

McMurrin, Mary (7), daughter, birthplace Scotland

McMurrin, Jenet (or Janet) (1), daughter, birthplace Scotland

McMurrin, Margaret (61), birthplace Scotland

McMurrin, Isabella (17), daughter, birthplace Scotland

Mitchell, Henry (41), birthplace England, laborer

Mitchell, Hariet (or Harriet) (46), birthplace England

Newman, Henry J. (27), husband, birthplace England, tinman

Newman, Maria A. (26), wife, birthplace England

Newman, Maria L. (4), daughter, birthplace England

Newman, Henry J. (3), son, birthplace England

Newman, Priscilla (1), daughter, birthplace England

Parker, Thomas (30), husband, birthplace England, ironmonger

Parker, Elizabeth J. (30), wife, birthplace England

Parker, Thomas J. (7), son, birthplace England

Parker, Elizabeth A. (4), daughter, birthplace England

Parker, Olive F. (2), daughter, birthplace England

Parker, Edith U. (6 months), daughter, birthplace England

Parry, Thomas (21), birthplace Wales, died August 13 of inflammation of the brain

Paul, William (27), birthplace England, joiner

Paul, Georgiana (27), birthplace England

Pay, Richard (35), husband, birthplace England, shoemaker

Pay, Sarah (30), wife, birthplace England, died October 4 at Chimney Rock

Pay, Marinda (or Marietta) Nancy, daughter, birthplace England, born July 11, died November 27

Petty, Edward (53), birthplace England, lawyer

Player, Elizabeth A. (17), birthplace Wales, dressmaker

Player, Emily (15), birthplace Wales

Power, Alois (25), birthplace Switzerland, wagonmaker

Price, John (36), husband, birthplace Wales, miner, marshal

Price, Margaret (23), wife, birthplace Wales

Price, John W. (4), son, birthplace Wales

Price, Baby Girl, born October 30 near Platte River

Price, Samuel (18), birthplace England, painter

Quinney, Mary A. (23), birthplace England

Reading, Ida (24), birthplace England

Reece (or Reese), James (60), birthplace England, farmer, died November 11, three days after leaving Devil's Gate

Reece, James (26), birthplace England, blacksmith

Reece, Mary (21), birthplace England

Rees, Ann (38), birthplace Wales

Routledge, Jassamine (or Jassemine) Elizabeth

Rowe, Charlotte (33), mother, birthplace England

Rowe, Robert W. (10), son, birthplace England

Rowe, Charlotte J. (8), birthplace England

Salisbury, William (39), husband, birthplace England, carpenter

Salisbury, Ann (37), wife, birthplace England

Salisbury, William (14), son, birthplace England

Salisbury, Henry (12), son, birthplace England

Salisbury, Joseph (4), son, birthplace England

Sinnatt, George (40), birthplace Wales, farmer

Sinnatt, Martha (46), wife

Smith, James (29), husband, birthplace England, clerk

Smith, Mary J. (29), wife, birthplace England

Smith, Frank P. (or Frank O.) (3), son, birthplace England

Smith, Edward W. (2), son, England

Smith, Alfred (18), birthplace England

Smith, Mary (64), mother, birthplace England

Smith, Robert (32), son, birthplace England, machine filler

Smith, Emma (26), daughter, birthplace England

Smith, Hester E. (9), daughter, birthplace England

Smith, Sarah A. (22), birthplace England

Spencer, George, Captain of 10

Spencer (or Schoonover), Gilbert (28), Captain of 10

Spicer, William (30), birthplace England

Spicer, Elizabeth (30), birthplace England

Standing (or Standring), Robert (23), birthplace England, laborer

Stephenson, Joshua (20), birthplace England, surgical instrument maker

Stock, Hester (or Esther) (19), birthplace South Africa

Strut (or Street), Amelia (62), birthplace England

Summers, Edwin (23), birthplace England, laborer, stayed at Devil's Gate

Taxford (or Tuxford), Sarah (29), birthplace U.S.

Thomas, Thomas (41), birthplace Wales, carpenter, Captain of 10

Thomas, William (51), birthplace Wales, farmer

Thorten, John B. (20), birthplace England, stone layer

Tripp, Margaret (23), birthplace England

Turner, John (43), father, birthplace England, farmer, died October 6, shortly before Scottsbluff, Nebraska

Turner, John (12), son, birthplace England, died November 16, between Devil's Gate and South Pass

Turner, Sophia (14), daughter, birthplace England, died November 12, four days past Devil's Gate

Van Schoonhoven, Gilbert, assistant to Captain Hunt

Wadsworth, Elizabeth (50), birthplace England

Wadsworth, James (8), birthplace England

Wadsworth, James (48), birthplace England, miner

Walters, John (47), birthplace Wales, tailor

Walters, Hester (or Esther) (39), wife, birthplace Wales, died October 7, when oxen attached to broken yoke stampeded

Walters, Adelaide (6), daughter, birthplace Wales

Walters, Jane, daughter, born September 6 at Shell Creek, Nebraska, died November 5, just before Independence Rock

Whitaker, John, birthplace England, laborer, stayed at Devil's Gate

White, Mary Ann Syer, mother, birthplace England, also had married daughter Eliza in the Hunt company

White, Elizabeth (18), daughter, birthplace England

White, Bernard (or Barnard) (16), son, birthplace England

White, Richard (13), son, birthplace England

Whitehead, Richard (47), husband, birthplace England, coppersmith

Whitehead, Elizabeth Walsh (52), wife, birthplace England

Whitehead, Jane (20), daughter, birthplace England

Whitehead, Margaret (18), daughter, birthplace England

Williams, Emily (17), birthplace England

Williams, Jane (12 or 19), birthplace Wales

Wiseman, John (54), birthplace England, surgeon

Wiseman, Mary Ann (42), birthplace England

Wiseman, John S. (or John Joseph) (5), birthplace England, died October 9

Wiseman, Henry H. (2), birthplace England, died August 30 at Florence, Nebraska

HODGETT WAGON COMPANY

The following names, ages in May of 1856, and birthplaces have been taken from Leroy R. Hafen and Ann W. Hafen, Handcarts to Zion, 1856–1860 (Glendale, Calif.: The Arthur H. Clark Co., 1960), pp. 289–94; 11/9/1856; and Susan Easton Black, Membership of The Church of Jesus Christ of Latter-day Saints, 1830–1848 (Provo, Utah: Brigham Young University Religious Studies Center, 1989), pp. 1–41. Discrepancies and names from other sources are also listed. In this and all other lists, birth and death dates are in 1856 unless specified otherwise.

The following names, ages, and birthplaces have been taken from Journal History of The Church of Jesus Christ of Latter-day Saints (Archives, LDS Church Historical Department, Salt Lake City, Utah), reports of the Hodgett wagon company on October 15, 1856, pp. 2–3 and December 15, 1856, pp. 2–37. Discrepancies and names from other sources are also listed.

From Iowa City, Iowa, to Salt Lake City, Utah:

Ahmansen, Grethe L. (or Grethe S.) (25), birthplace Norway

Ahmansen, Jacob A. (1), birthplace Norway

Ammon, Sarah (30), birthplace U.S.

Andersen (or Anderson), Anders (20), birthplace Denmark

Andersen, Jorgen (20), birthplace Denmark

Ayrton, Isabella (54), birthplace England, died en route

Aryton, William (26), birthplace England

Ballan, William (39), birthplace England. William is not grouped and family on Journal Roster, but Ann is called wife, not mother, so it is assumed they are married

Ballan, Ann (41), wife, birthplace England

Ballan, Charles W. (17), son, birthplace England

Ballan, Sarah Ann R. (8), daughter, birthplace England

Bettel (or Bithel), Samuel (19), birthplace England

Boden, Mary (21), birthplace England

Bond, William (39), father, birthplace England

Bond, Mary Ann (34), wife, birthplace England

Bond, Sarah (17), birthplace England

Bond, Ann (15), birthplace England

Bond, John (12), birthplace England

Bond, Margaret (8), birthplace England

Bond, Mary Ann or Mary Jane (6), birthplace England

Bond, Joseph William (3), birthplace England

Bond, Nephi Alma (1), birthplace England

Burnham, Elizabeth (21), birthplace England

Callan, Charles W., birthplace England

Callan, Ann

Christensen, Christian (11), birthplace Denmark

Christensen, Lars (24), birthplace Denmark

Cooper, John (22), birthplace England, engaged to and traveling with Mary Ann Lewis, stayed at Devil's Gate

Crowsa (Krause), Wilhelmine (8), birthplace Denmark

Dove, James (37), husband, birthplace England

Dove, Alice (39), wife, birthplace England

Dove, George (14), son, birthplace England

Dove, Sarah (12), daughter, birthplace England

Fisher, William (42), birthplace England

Fisher, Elizabeth (33), birthplace England

Gadd (or Gade), Frederik C. H. (25), birthplace Denmark

Gillies, Ann S., birthplace England

Gillies, Christina G., birthplace England

Gillies, Daniel S., birthplace England

Gillies, Robert (35), birthplace Scotland

Gillies, Jane (35), birthplace Scotland

Gillies, Moroni (10), birthplace Scotland

Gillies, Ann (9), birthplace Scotland

Gillies, Daniel (7), birthplace Scotland

Gillies, Christian (3), birthplace Scotland

Gillies, Robert, birthplace Denmark. One list has this family in the Willie company

Gillies, Jean Ann

Gillies, Baby Girl

Goler (or Golder), Richard (24), birthplace England

Goler, Mary Ann (20), birthplace England

Goler, Heber (20), relationship unknown, birthplace England

Goler, Emma (2), birthplace England

Goler, George (4 months), birthplace England

Goodsall (or Godsall or Godsell), John (47), father, birthplace England, Chaplain of Hodgett company

Goodsall, Mary (52), wife, birthplace England

Goodsall, Louisa (19), daughter, birthplace England

Goodsall, Susan (16), daughter, birthplace England

Goodsall, Francey (or Frances) (8), daughter, birthplace England

Goodsall, John J. (5), son, birthplace England

Gourley, Robert (17), son of Paul Gourley in Martin handcart company, birthplace Scotland

Gourley, Alexander (15), son of Paul Gourley in Martin handcart company, birthplace Scotland

Haines, George (19)

Hamilton, Henry (24), birthplace Scotland

Haven, Jesse, birthplace U.S.

Hawkins, William (39), husband, birthplace England

Hawkins, Elizabeth (40), wife, birthplace England

Higgs, George, birthplace U.S.

Higgs, Thomas (33), father, birthplace England

Higgs, Elizabeth Stowe (31), mother, birthplace England

Higgs, Mary Susanna (or Mary Suzanne) (7), daughter, birthplace England

Higgs, Ann C. (or Ann Elizabeth) (2), daughter

Hill, Mary (59 or 48), birthplace England

Hodgett, Emily (15), sister, birthplace England

Hodgett, William Benjamin (24), Captain of company, brother, birthplace England, returning from mission to Great Britain

Jackson, Joseph (42), birthplace England

Jensen (or Yensen), Christian (or Christen) (30), birthplace Denmark

Jensen (or Yensen), Karen (38), birthplace Denmark

Jensen (or Yensen), Christen (or Jens C.) (1), birthplace Denmark

Jensen, Stene (17)

Jerry, Joseph, birthplace England

Jones, William (45)

Jones, Mary Ann (49)

Jones, Robert (21)

Jones, Louisa (19)

Jones, Frederick (14)

Jorgensen, Lars (41), birthplace Denmark

Jorgensen, Karen C. (30), birthplace Denmark

Jorgensen, Karen (3), birthplace Denmark

Kasmase, K., birthplace Denmark

Kouslett, Jessimine (or Jessemine) (20), birthplace England

Lanesen, T., birthplace Denmark

Larsen, Niels (30), birthplace Denmark

Larson (or Larsen), John (27), birthplace Denmark

Larson, John (32), husband, birthplace Denmark

Larson, Anna (29), wife, birthplace Denmark

Larson, Christiana M. (5), daughter, birthplace Denmark

Larson, Sarah (3), daughter, birthplace Denmark

Larson, Lanthe (1), birthplace Denmark

Lason (or Larson), Line (or Lene) (50), birthplace Denmark

Latey, Henry (17), birthplace England

Latey, John (21)

Leisley, Alice (61), widow, birthplace England

Leisley, Ann (24), daughter, birthplace England

Lewis, Mary Ann (22), birthplace England, engaged to and traveling with John Cooper

Lund, Hans C. (28), birthplace Denmark

Lund, Nielsine Kreutzbach (35), wife, birthplace Denmark

Lund, Hans Christian (or Hans L.) (8), son, birthplace Denmark

Lund, Nielsine Wilhelmine (2), daughter, birthplace Denmark

Madsen, Lars (62), husband, birthplace Denmark, died en route

Madsen, Bodil (50), wife, birthplace Denmark

Madsen, Lars Christian (8), son, birthplace Denmark

Manning, Elisha A. (21), birthplace U.S.; stayed at Devil's Gate

Mason, Brother, birthplace Denmark

Mason, Boy, son, birthplace Denmark

Mekelsen (or Mekelser or Mickelsen or Mikkelsen), Ole (or C.) (42), birthplace Denmark

Mikkelsen, Maren (61)

More, John H., birthplace Ireland

Neilsen (or Nielsen), Johanne (26), birthplace Denmark

Neilsen (or Nielsen), Maren (32), birthplace Denmark

Nilson, Anna (29), birthplace Denmark

Nilson, Eliza (or Lissa or Sissa) (22), birthplace Sweden

Olsen, Christian (54), birthplace Norway

Otesen (or Otsen or Olsen), Hans (22), birthplace Denmark

Perry, Joseph (20), birthplace England

Peterson, Anna (20), birthplace Denmark

Philip, (or Phillip or Philips or Phillips), Alfred (27), birthplace England

Porter, Nathan Tanner (36), Captain of 10, birthplace U.S.

Provost, Luke (40), father, birthplace U.S.

Provost, Julia Ann (40), birthplace U.S.

Provost, Julia Ann (22), birthplace U.S.

Provost, Charles B. (20), birthplace U.S.

Provost, James Wheeler (12), birthplace U.S.

Provost, David Woodruff (6), birthplace U.S.

Provost, Sarah Catherine (2), birthplace U.S.

Rasmasen (or Rasmussen), Hans (22), birthplace Denmark

Rasmasen (or Rasmussen), Hans (40), husband, birthplace Denmark

Rasmasen, Maren (35), wife, birthplace Denmark

Rasmasen, Rasmus (11), son, birthplace Denmark

Rasmasen, Jens (9), son, birthplace Denmark

Rasmasen, Bertha (or Benth) (7), daughter, birthplace Denmark

Rasmasen, Karen (4), daughter, birthplace Denmark

Rasmasen, Anna (2), daughter, birthplace Denmark

Roper, Charles (37), Captain of 10, birthplace England

Roper, Catherine (28), birthplace England

Rowley (or Rowly), John (33), husband, birthplace England; brother to George and James

Rowley, Isabella (33), wife, birthplace England

Rowley, William (12), son, birthplace England

Rowley, Isabella, (9), daughter, birthplace England

Rowley, Sarah (6), daughter, birthplace England

Rowley, Joseph (5), son, birthplace England

Rowley, Margrett (or Margaret) (4), daughter, birthplace England

Rowley, Mary (2), daughter, birthplace England

Rowley (or Rowly), George (28), brother, birthplace England, died on plains

Rowley, James (23), brother, birthplace England

S., Ann, this sister is recorded on October 15 roster but not on December 15 roster

Scott, Mary (39), widow, birthplace U.S.

Scott, Joseph (4), son, birthplace U.S.

Senior, Thomas (25), birthplace England

Slater, Thomas (26), birthplace England

Soresen (or Sorensen), Martha (65 or 62), birthplace Denmark

Sterly (or Starley), Henry (31), birthplace England, died en route

Stewart, William (or James) (28), husband, birthplace Scotland, cabinet maker; family also listed by DUP in Martin handcart company

Stewart, Elizabeth Murdoch (32), wife, birthplace Scotland, died November 23

Stewart, James Murdoch (4), son

Stewart, William, son, died in Florence

Stewart, Niel Murdoch (1), son

Stewart, Elizabeth, daughter, born October 23, died three days later

Swenson, John (27), birthplace Sweden, Captain of 10

Taylor, Sarah (20), birthplace England; her mother and family were traveling in Martin handcart company

Tenant, Thomas (46), birthplace England, wealthy benefactor of British Saints, died en route

Tenant, Jane (24), wife, birthplace England

Tenant, Thomas (1), son, birthplace England

Upton, William (34), died October 23, of mortification of the heart, fifteen miles past Fort Bridger

Vernon, Joseph (37), husband, birthplace Wales

Vernon, Ann (32), wife, birthplace Wales

Watt, George (19), birthplace England; stayed at Devil's Gate

Williams, Amelia (52 or 32), birthplace England

Williams, Ann (or Ann Kite Stowe) (16 or 66), birthplace England

RESCUERS

The following individuals are listed as rescuers of the Willie and Martin handcart companies in Rebecca Bartholomew and Leonard J. Arrington, Rescue of the 1856 Handcart Companies (Provo, Utah: Brigham Young University, Charles Redd Center for Western Studies, 1992). Discrepancies and names from other sources are also listed.

Alexander, Thomas Murphy (26), main rescue party; stayed at Devil's Gate to help guard the cache

Allen, Frank

Allred, Paulinas H.

Allred, Reddick N. (34), main rescue party; met Willie company near the Sweetwater on October 24, ascending Rocky Ridge

Alvord, Joseph B., rode in commissary wagon with Alice F. Bury Walsh and helped with her three small children after her husband died at Devil's Gate

Amussen, Captain

Atkinson, William

Bailey, John

Bankhead, Thomas, main rescue party

Barker, James

Barlow, Israel

Bean, George Washington

Beck, T. H.

Beckstead, Henry

Bell, William Milton

Bennett, Brother

Bennion, Samuel

Billingham, Daniel

Bingham, J.

Blackburn, Elias

Blackham, John

Blair, Brother, camped November 4 on other side of Bear River with three ox wagons; left company November 8, headed to Salt Lake Valley

Blair, Seth M.

Bowman, George, from Provo

Brimhall, Noah

Broomhead, William K., main rescue party

Brown, Abraham

Brown, Gurnsey, from Draper, helped Hunt company

Brown, Newel A.

Bullock, Isaac (32)

Bullock, Thomas

Burton, Robert T. (36), main rescue party. One source refers to a Richard Burton who was one of two Assistants to Captain Grant

Butler, Taylor

Call, Anson

Carter, William

Clawson, George from Draper, helped Hunt company

Cloward, Jack

Cluff, Harvey H. (20), main rescue party

Cole, James, married Lucy Ward November 2, west of Fort Bridger

Cole, Moroni

Condie, Gibson

Cornia, Peter

Cousins, Samuel

Cowley, William M. (Miller)

Crandall, Martin

Davis, James

Dawson, William, from Lehi, helped Hodgett company into Salt Lake from Fort Bridger

Decker, Charles Franklin (32), was appointed guide for main rescue party

Devenish, Henry

Driggs, Benjamin W.

Dunn, George

Dunn, Jimmy

Dunyon, John

Ekins, John, met Martin handcart company at Echo Canyon; his sister, Sarah R. Ekins Walker, was a member of the Martin company

Elder, Joseph

Ellis, Joseph

Ensign, Rufus Bronson

Ensign, Lorine

Fairbanks, Amos, main rescue party

Farmer, James

Ferguson (or Furguson), James (28), spoke at Iowa City camp on July 4

Follett, Brother

Foss, Brother

Fuller, Sanford

Gardner, Elias

Garr, Abel, main rescue party, and sons

Garr, David

Garr, John

Gibbs, Gideon D.

Goldsbrough, Henry, main rescue party

Gould, Brother, appointed Captain of horse teams on November 3

Grant, George D. (40), and son, Captain of the main rescue party, met Willie company on October 21 with supplies

Grant, George W. (18), main rescue party, one of those who carried members of Martin company over the Sweetwater

Grant, Lewis McKeachie

Grey, Charles, main rescue party

Haight, William Van Orden

Hamilton, Ben, stayed at Devil's Gate to help guard the cache

Hampton, Benjamin (19), main rescue party

"Handsome Cupid," so listed by Dan Jones; identity unproven

Hanks, Ephraim K. (29), passed Willie camp fifteen miles west of Green River; brought news of more rescuers on November 2

Harvey, John

Hawley, Asa (21)

Haws, Albert, from Provo

Hinckley, Arza

Hogan, Goudy (27)

Horne, Henry James

Hunting, Nathan

Huntington, C. Allen (18), main rescue party, one of those who carried members of Martin company over the Sweetwater

Huntington, Oliver

Hyde, William, appointed Captain of ox teams November 3 at Muddy Creek

Ivie, James (26)

Ivins, Israel (Corbett)

Jack, James

Johnson, Daniel

Jones, Daniel W. (26), main rescue party; reports that he was appointed Chief Cook; stayed at Devil's Gate

Jones, William Robert

Judd, Riley

Kimball, David Patton (18), main rescue party, and two brothers; one of those who carried members of Martin company over the Sweetwater

Kimball, Heber Parley (21)

Kimball, William Henry (31), main rescue party, returning missionary to England; one of two Assistants to Captain Grant, he met the Willie company October 21 with supplies

Knights, Gates A.

Lee, Edward

Lee, Edwin

Linton, Samuel (29)

Little, Feramorz (36)

Lott, John S.

Maddison, John F.

Matson, George B.

Maxfield, Elijah

Maycock, Amos

McAllister, John D. T.

McDonald, John

McDonnell, Henry

McKenzie, George

McLelland, Thomas

Merrill, George G.

Miles, E. R.

Mills, W. G., married Emily Hill, a member of Martin handcart company

Moss, John

Mott, Daniel

Moulton, Charles Alma

Murdock, John Riggs (30), main rescue party

Nebeker, Ira (17), main rescue party

Newell, Horace

Nowlan, C.

Osborn, Dave

Packard, Milan

Parker, John, cared for and later married

Maria Jackson Normington of Martin handcart company

Parker, William, son, main rescue party

Parrish, Joel, main rescue party

Partington, William Edward

Partridge, Jonathan

Patten, George

Peck, Edwin (or Edward) Martin (28), main rescue party

Perkins, Brigham Young

Porter, Lyman Wight

Pulsipher, William

Pulsipher, John

Rhodes, Alonzo D., from Lehi, helped Hodgett company into Salt Lake from Fort Bridger

Rice, Oscar

Richardson, Ebenezer

Ricks, Thomas Edwin (28), main rescue party

Roberts, William D.

Robison, Lewis

Roundy, Loren

Russell, H. M.

Sanders, Brother

Sanderson, Henry W.

Sevy, George

Shupe, James Wright (33)

Simmons, Joseph Marcellus (22)

Simmons, William Bert, drove a wagon in which Mary Taylor Upton, a member of Martin handcart company, rode; he later married her

Skeen, John, from Lehi, helped Hodgett company into Salt Lake from Fort Bridger

Skeens, Joseph

Slater, Thomas

Smith, Joseph F. (Miller)

Smith, Lot, helped rescue Martin handcart company

Smith, William B.
Soper, Richard
Spafford, William Nelson
Spencer, Claudious Victor or C. N.
Spencer, George
Spencer, Hiram Theron
Sperry, Harrison
Standley, Franklin (25)
Stanton, D. W.
Steed, Thomas, had niece, Sarah Steed, in Willie company
Stout, Hosea (46)
Streeper, William Henry
Stringham, George
Summers, George
Sumsion, William
Talcott, Brother
Taylor, Stephen Wells (22), also listed with middle initial H., main rescue party; one of those who carried members of Martin company over Sweetwater
Teeples, Sidney (19), drove a team to help rescue the Martin handcart company; he later married a member of the Martin company, Nicholus Gourley
Terry, Joshua

Thomas, Brother, went to Salt Lake Valley with W. H. Kimball on November 4 to report conditions of companies
Tidwell, Peter
Tracy, Mosiah
Van Cott, John (42), returning President of Scandinavian Mission
Wachman, H. H.
Wadsworth, Abiah
Warren, William
Webb, Chauncey G., main rescue party, returning handcart agent in Iowa
Webb, Edward Milo, son of Chauncey Webb, at Green River
Wheelock, Angus
Wheelock, Cyrus Hubbard (43), chaplain of main rescue party
Whitbeck, John
Whitman, Brother
Whitney, John
Wickersham, John
Wilken, David
Wilkens, Brother
Williams, Alexander
Williams, James V.
Wilson, H. W., from Provo
Wilson, Robert

Wilson, Thomas Henry
Winn, Dennis (24), from Salt Lake City, who had a mother and sister in the Martin handcart company; he later discovered his mother had died
Winn, William H.
Winward, Peter
Woolley, Franklin
Woolley, Henry
Workman, Albert
Young, Brigham, Jr. (20), and brother, he helped keep Big and Little Mountain roads open for the handcart companies
Young, Joseph A. (22), main rescue party, returning missionary to England

Some brethren were stationed near Rock Creek on October 25 with supplies for company.
The Willie company met seven wagons from Fort Supply on October 31 west of Green River.
The Willie company met another three wagons from the Salt Lake Valley on October 31.
The Willie company met several teams from the Salt Lake Valley on November 1.
Several teams from the Valley picked up the sick west of Fort Bridger on November 2.
Several wagons from the Valley came to help on November 3.
Ten ox teams headed east to meet Martin company, passed Willie on November 3 near Muddy Creek.
Several teams passed Willie company on November 4 headed east to other companies.
Some teams passed Willie company on November 7 near Cottonwood Grove, headed east to relieve other companies.
Not all the names of the rescuers were recorded.

INDEX